More Praise for
Schools Cannot Do It Alone

"Vollmer provides a new understanding of the complex issues we face. His captivating story shows how we can work together to help our schools and communities meet the demands of a rapidly changing society."
— *Gerald N. Tirozzi, Executive Director, National Association of Secondary School Principals*

"With fresh eyes, Jamie helps us see and feel how the permeating culture within our schools is tied to public attitudes and beliefs. His strategy for change is just what today's educators and their allies need to build an authentic conversation about increasing student success."
— *Rich Bagin, Executive Director, National School Public Relations Association*

"It is true, schools *cannot* do it alone. Jamie offers every community an opportunity to develop successful models for student and school success."
— *Chuck Saylors, President, National PTA*

"Jamie Vollmer understands the need to create schools where every child's potential is realized, and he is realistic about the barriers that hold us back. This book provides a blueprint for every community to unite around a common purpose and unleash the full potential of its citizens to realize our dreams."
— *Jim Lynch, Executive Director, Association of Wisconsin School Administrators*

"Excellent work! The true challenge for public schools is the increasing rate of change. Just when we have restructured in response to No Child Left Behind, along comes Race To The Top, and off we go. *Schools Cannot Do It Alone* provides practical tools that any educator can use to rally the entire community to work together to increase student success."
— *Peter Ansingh, Superintendent, West Valley School District Yakima, WA*

"Mr. Vollmer's work confirms that it's not great principals or great teachers alone who are the keys to educating all children to high levels. It is the work of those people, plus the understanding, trust, and support of our communities that will allow us to meet our goals."
— *Brady Link, Superintendent, Christian County Schools, President, Kentucky Association of School Superintendents*

"From the opening pages, I was mesmerized by this book and Vollmer's common sense approach to the issues surrounding American public education."
— *Mary A. Francis, Executive Director, Alaska Council of School Administrators*

Praise for Jamie's Presentations

"How good was he? At the end of his presentation, there were long lines at the bathrooms because no one wanted to get up during his address. There can be no higher praise than that!"

—High school teacher, Verona, WI

"I have never seen a veteran staff, or any staff, give a standing ovation to an Opening Day presenter. Jamie made them feel like they were doing a good job, and, at the same time, he challenged them to continue to improve."

—Frank House, Superintendent,
South Lewis Central Schools, Turin, NY

"He does it every time! Everyone loved it. Everyone got something they could use."

—Bruce Hunter, Assoc. Exec. Dir.,
American Assn. of School Administrators

"A home run! Jamie was the right man, at the right time, with the right message."

—Jim Puckett, Executive Dir.,
Georgia Assn of Educational Leaders

"I was mesmerized. What a GREAT way to start the school year! Mr. Vollmer was hilarious, engaging, and inspirational. I wanted to run up and hug him for valuing us and what we do."

—Middle school teacher, San Juan Capistrano, CA

"Appropriate. Dynamic. Informative. His presentation was exceptional, and he was a pleasure to work with."

—Jeff Dema, Chairman,
Economic Development Council, Clay County, KS

"His words at our Partnership Luncheon were truly passionate and inspiring. The audience wanted more!"

—J. Tim Mills, Superintendent,
Mesa County District 51, Grand Junction, CO

"His interactive approach with the audience was quite effective. His message was loud and clear: educators have to get the word out to the community about our success."

—Sheryl Solow, Dir. of Staff Development, Bucks County, PA Intermediate Unit

"He really struck a cord with the audience. He got a standing ovation from a group that does not give standing ovations."

—Gary Markenson, Executive Director,
Missouri Municipal League

SCHOOLS CANNOT DO IT ALONE

Building public support
for America's public schools

Jamie Vollmer

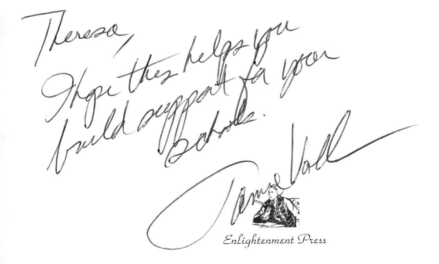

Theresa,
I hope this helps you
build support for your
schools.

Jamie Voll

Enlightenment Press

Enlightenment Press
1978 Cherry Tree Lane
Fairfield IA, 52556

First Enlightenment Press paperback edition July 2010.

For information about special discounts for bulk purchases,
please contact sales@schoolscannotdoitalone.com.

To invite Jamie Vollmer to speak at your event
please call 1-641-472-1558
or visit www.schoolscannotdoitalone.com.

Library of Congress Control Number: 2010927915
ISBN: 978-0-982-7569-0-4
Printed in the United States of America

TO MY FATHER

He was the best teacher I ever had,
but I don't think I ever told him.

Contents

PART III. The Public Is Not Ready

PART IV. The Great Conversation

Contents

Introduction

M y father died in a spectacular room in his home on the Florida coast. Three walls of glass gave sweeping views of a white sand beach and aquamarine sea. In his final days, his hospital bed was placed against the eastern wall so ocean and sky were all he could see. Propped up by pillows, resting warm in the sun, he sat as though he were on the deck of a great ship surrounded by rolling waves.

Dad loved that room, but I was glad to be out of it. In an hour, I would deliver his eulogy. I needed a place to steady my heart and collect my thoughts. His private office at the back of the house was the place to be.

All the honors, awards, and souvenirs of his life were on display in that still, paneled room. I had known many of these keepsakes since I was a boy. His Phi Beta Kappa key sat in a glass case. His Ph.D. diploma hung on the wall. Industrial rubies and emeralds lay beside a scale model of the first Lunar Lander, reminders of his work with lasers in the early days of the space program. Desk drawers held dozens of patents and volumes of published papers. A diploma from the Harvard Business School announced his midlife transition from physics to management, and the bookshelves held plaques, testimonials, and photos that bore witness to his subsequent rise to the highest levels of corporate power.

Every one of these tokens had a story attached, and there was a time when I could recount them all. But as I sat alone in the quiet, I could feel the details slipping away. I remembered an old Ethiopian proverb: When an old man dies, a great library burns.

Now, I knew what it meant.

There was one story, however, that I could never forget.

Prominently displayed on his desk were photographs of all the people closest to his heart. (I was happy to see that I'd made the cut.) Positioned among the pictures of our extended family was a photo of an apple-cheeked woman with piercing blue eyes. With her broad smile, silver hair, and lavender jacket, she evoked the Queen Mother. She was not part of our family, but I had known her my whole life. Her name was Miss Katherine J. Skelton. She was my dad's fourth grade teacher, and their story sits at the heart of this book.

My father attended public school during the Great Depression in a poor Philadelphia neighborhood. By all accounts, he was not much of a student in his early years. Unruly, inattentive, unproductive; a regular on the principal's bench. Not angry or mean, just not interested. At the end of the third grade, his teacher suggested that he was "slow." My grandparents vehemently rejected the idea, but they were ill equipped to respond. They had little education, and, like their neighbors, they were struggling just to survive. Little Jimmy Vollmer was on his own.

Then came fourth grade.

I have no idea how much the story has been embellished over the years. All I know for sure is that something happened. How many grown men have a picture of their fourth grade teacher on their desks? Miss Skelton saw something in my father that others had missed.

The third grade teacher had warned her, "Watch out for the squirmy redhead." And so she did. Miss Skelton watched out for my dad for the next nine years. She worked with him after school. She pressed him beyond the normal assignments. She exposed him to the world outside his poor neighborhood. She let him know that he had the potential to do anything he wanted. He could rise above his environment. He could go to college. He could be great. With her help, he became the school's best student and president of his senior class. He was awarded a full scholarship to the University of Pennsylvania. He earned both a bachelor's and a master's degree, served in the Navy during WWII, and married a beautiful Italian girl from Schenectady, NY. They had two boys and a girl. In 1956, he successfully defended his Ph.D. dissertation, and began his career.

Fifty years later, my father died surrounded by love and luxury. Accomplished, admired, and respected.

One might suppose that he had exceeded Miss Skelton's expectations. But, in delivering *her* eulogy in 1997, Dad declared that Katherine had seen it all long before he had any notion of the possibilities. "There were," he said with a slight tremor in his voice, "things on her list that I have yet to accomplish. In my life, Katherine Skelton was the difference."

The most extraordinary thing about this story is that it is not extraordinary. The magnitude of my father's success may be striking, but in America's *public* schools, the basics of this story are repeated every day. Millions of Ms, Mrs., and Mr. Skeltons encounter tens of millions of squirmy Jimmy Vollmers with all their problems and potential. These teachers see the possibilities and strive to help their students succeed, often in environments that test their sanity.

I emphasize public schools not because I have anything against private schools. They play an important role in America's education establishment. If nothing else, they prove that parental involvement, smaller classes, minimal red tape, motivated students, and, sometimes, more money result in higher student achievement. Many private school leaders and their staffs do excellent work, and I hope that they find much within this book that is useful. But public education is the miracle.

Public schools broke the link between accidents of birth and access to education that determined the social order for centuries. Public schools unleashed the creative intelligence of tens of millions of children both privileged and disenfranchised. Public education made our democracy possible and powered our ascent to global preeminence. America is the first country on the planet to aggressively pursue publicly funded, equal educational opportunity for all, and the return on our investment has been glorious.

This book is unabashedly written in support of public education and its remarkable employees. It is not, however, a defense of the status quo. Our schools must change. They were designed to serve a society that no longer exists.

The industrial era has given way to the knowledge age and every aspect of American life is being transformed. The two-tiered world of work has all but disappeared, blurring the lines between jobs for the head and jobs for the hand. Initiative, creative thinking, and problem solving are now encouraged if not required at every level of employment. On the job and at home, success now rests on our ability to continually learn and apply what we have learned to a constantly changing array of problems. Americans, young and old, confront complex issues related to law, medicine, personal finance, ethics, privacy, security, and politics; everyone must have the skills to sort fact from fiction, and truth from lies, opinion, and hype. For the first time in history, our security, our prosperity, and the health of our nation depend upon our ability to unfold the full creative potential of every child. Not just the easy ones, not just the top twenty-five percent of the class.

Our schools were not designed to do this. They were built to *select and sort* students into two groups: a small handful of thinkers and a great mass of obedient doers. They were created, as Thomas Jefferson said in his *Notes on the State of Virginia, 1781–2*, "to rake the geniusses from the rubbish." In the 220 years since the great man introduced his plan, armies of ardent reformers have strengthened, streamlined, and standardized his basic design. Their cumulative efforts have produced the schools we have today—public *and* private. Schools in which we hold time constant, even though every teacher, administrator, and parent knows that some children take longer to learn than others. Schools in which we favor certain profiles of intelligence over those we deem less valuable. Schools where we sort the winners from losers not based on their capacity to learn, but on their ability to perform within the strictures of school. Schools where teachers and administrators are forced to become subversives in order to do their best work.

An argument can be made that the selecting process was practical in an age when the pace of change was slow, options were limited, and only a small handful of people were paid to think. But it was never moral. And today, it is neither moral nor practical. Our schools must change.

I want to be crystal clear. I am talking about a systems problem, not a people problem. Most teachers will admit that they can improve, and we must surround them with high quality programs of professional development. But the truth is that most of America's Pre-K-12 educators are smart, dedicated professionals doing everything they can to ensure that their students succeed in school and in life. They are not the primary problem.

I did not always believe this. Once, I strongly believed that the "insiders" were the obstacles to change. But in the twenty years since I stumbled into the education arena from the world of business, I have watched them work in scores of schools. America's teachers spend more hours per day in front of their classes than their peers anywhere in the industrialized world. They juggle their disparate tasks before audiences comprised of diverse, distracted, demanding children, many of whom are victims of a pop culture that overstimulates their physiologies, fractures their attention spans, and promotes a bizarre sense of entitlement. Principals are asked to be both efficient branch managers and brilliant instructional leaders; they have become the shock absorbers of the system—squeezed by directives from above and demands from below. Superintendents and their administrative teams spend their days (and nights) attempting to stretch insufficient resources to meet rising expectations. They struggle to balance competing public and private interests while being denounced for earning salaries that no private sector CEO managing a comparable organization would even consider. And everyone who works in our schools labors to respond to the consequences of "mandate creep": the ever-expanding list of academic, social, medical, psychological, and nutritional responsibilities that has been crammed into an academic calendar that has not grown by a single minute in decades.

A forty-hour workweek for these people is nothing. Fifty hours, sixty hours, is routine. But every teacher and administrator could work a hundred hours and we would still not produce the graduates we need. No matter how hard they work, no matter how often they are threatened, they cannot teach all children to high levels in a system designed to teach only some. The problem is not the people. It's the system. Confusing the two is a terrible mistake that politicians, business leaders, academics, bureaucrats, media pundits, and even educators have made for decades. Misidentifying the core problem has cost American taxpayers billions of dollars and America's educators untold hours of wasted effort. Most troubling, it has cost millions of young Americans the opportunity to succeed.

Public education must be aggressively supported if America is to remain great, but the system must be changed.

It cannot, however, change in isolation. You cannot touch a school without touching the culture of the surrounding town. Everything that goes on inside our schools is fused, in some transcendental way, to the local community's attitudes, opinions, values, and beliefs. This is the one true thing I have learned in the twenty years of pressing for change. And I learned it the hard way.

Again and again, I watched communities reject reforms not because they were irrational, but because they offended local sensibilities. I saw smart, progressive superintendents and their boards mount valiant campaigns to improve student success only to be rebuked and sometimes fired because their plans conflicted with the community's notions of "real school." Over time, I was forced to accept an undeniable, albeit daunting fact: to meet the challenges of the knowledge age, to unfold the full creative potential of every child, we must do more than change our schools, we must change America, one community at a time. The question was, how?

I searched for an answer in the field. I visited hundreds of schools and spoke to thousands of educators and community members who were attempting to effect substantive change. I witnessed false starts and bloody battles. And with each new experience, I saw more clearly the enormity of the task.

I also became sensitive to the damage caused by the unrelenting stream of negativity directed at our schools. I am not talking about honest criticism. Public education is huge and bureaucratic with deep cultural roots. It needs outside pressure to improve. I refer to the practice of bashing public schools as a blood sport: a dangerous game in which self-serving politicians portray public schools as dismal failures that they alone can fix, and media pundits blame schools for social ills over which they have no control; a game where false comparisons are made between past and present, public and private, us versus them; where headlines broadcast half-truths, statistics are used out of context, and test results are reported in the worst possible light.

I confess there were moments when I doubted the system could be changed. I experienced these moments of misgiving even though everything I saw in the global economy confirmed, beyond a reasonable doubt, that we had no choice but to succeed. It was only after years of watching reform initiatives die in the planning that I perceived a path to progress.

I realized that something was missing in the standard approach to reform. It wasn't a lack of effort or conviction. There was no shortage of research, standards, accountability, or proven practical programs. It was deeper. There was something missing in the community, specifically in the school/community relationship. There was a dearth of certain intangible but essential resources: understanding, trust, permission, and support. I labeled these resources the Prerequisites of Progress, and, on reflection, it became obvious that they had to be developed *before* systemic transformation could occur.

It was a great relief to identify the problem. But it was an even greater relief to realize that the Prerequisites could be obtained through a single course of action: something practical that required no new money; something that could be easily implemented with existing personnel; something that promised enough tangible benefits to entice everyone on staff and all their allies in the community to participate.

I call it The Great Conversation. It's a strategically coherent, tactically sound, community-wide enterprise that any district can initiate and maintain. By adding this missing piece to their ongoing efforts to increase student success, school districts across the country can secure the Prerequisites of Progress, and, at the same time, inoculate the people of their communities against the ravages of viral negativity. I believe everyone can and should play a part in The Great Conversation, and the time to act is now. For this is public education's most hopeful time.

I know it can be hard to see from the trenches where the challenges seem to multiply by the hour, but a great opportunity lies before us. Public schools have never been more important. Every path to individual, community, and national success now runs through those classroom doors. For the first time in history, we must educate all children to high levels. Finally, social and economic conditions are right for all of us to come together and create public schools where all students can unfold their full creative potential and every member of the staff can fulfill his or her professional dreams.

We can speed our progress toward the realization of these cherished goals with a basic understanding of The Great Conversation and its immense benefits. With the story of my dad and Ms Skelton as my inspiration, and after years of working and learning in districts across the country, I am pleased to offer this understanding within the pages of this book.

PART I

From Critic to Ally

Chapter 1

Run It Like a Business!

He's as blind as he can be, just sees what he wants to see.

The Beatles

L ong before I understood the need for The Great Conversation, before I became an advocate for public schools, I was a critic, and not shy about it.

I entered the education arena in the fall of 1988. Earlier in the year, Dr. William Lepley, Iowa's Secretary of Education, invited me to serve on the Iowa Business and Education Roundtable. At the time, I was managing a manufacturing firm called The Great Midwestern Ice Cream Company. Three year before, we had become famous when *People* magazine—that fine research periodical—declared that our Blueberry ice cream was the "*Best Ice Cream In America*." Shortly thereafter, the *Chicago Tribune* called our Madagascar Vanilla "*Blessed*," and Jane Pauley of the "Today Show" inhaled a bowl of Black Raspberry on national TV. Articles praising our company appeared in *Time, Newsweek,* the *Wall Street Journal,* and the *New York Times.* There was even an anatomy magazine that said our ice cream was the best. It's true. It's called *Playboy.* I seem to recall it said something about our luscious scoops.

Life was good as an ice cream man. Everybody liked me, which was in stark contrast to my time spent as an attorney. I was the most popular father on the block. I was also the target of frequent requests for donations. So when Dr. Lepley called, I assumed that free ice cream was on the agenda. I was wrong.

Bill explained that the Roundtable was to be an independent group of private and public sector leaders formed to make recommendations for improving Iowa's schools. He said they could use my voice. I was flattered, but I was also very busy. I was hip deep in an election year publicity campaign that was generating huge press. We had created special flavors for every candidate running for president: Dole's Top Banana, Dukakis' Massachewy Chocolate, Bush's Preppy Mint, Pat Robertson's Devil's Food Swirl, Babbit's Cactus Cookie, and, of course, Gary Hart's Donna Rice Cream. I suggested to Bill that, perhaps, a donation of ten gallons of our sumptuous Cherry Vanilla would suffice. He thanked me for the offer—nobody ever turned it down—but he insisted that my experience in business would be an asset. His persistence caused me to waver, and he quickly added that he was only talking about three meetings a year, which proves that a decent and honest man can occasionally shade the truth. In retrospect, I cannot believe I bought it, but I accepted his invitation, and my life would never be the same.

I arrived at the first meeting armed with interest and enthusiasm and zero understanding of the issues. My only child was a toddler at the time. I had not stepped foot inside a school since I graduated in the 1960s. My opinions were largely based upon what I had read and heard in the popular media. I shared the dim view of public schools common among my peers. It seemed obvious that our schools were failing: an alarming gap had grown between what our students knew and what they needed to know. We were not getting the kind of workers we needed. We were falling behind our international competitors. Our way of life was at risk. Something needed to change.

I was convinced that we had a people problem. Unionized

teachers and overpaid administrators were the obstacles to progress. They were hunkered down in a monopoly, protected from the competitive pressures of the marketplace. They had no reason to change and no incentive to work hard. We had to raise productivity. We needed reforms that would turn up the heat by imposing accountability measures that rewarded success and punished failure. We needed to raise standards, demand rigor, reject excuses, and introduce competition.

Prior to that day, I had not met any of the other Roundtable members. By the end of the meeting, however, everyone on the business side of the table had bonded. We had all reached the same conclusion: to overcome the obstacles, we had to run schools like a business.

A Harvard professor, Dr. Lewis Perelman, was our first presenter. He was there to challenge our conceptions of the traditional model of school. He used words like "heuristic," "hyperlearning," and "paradigm," and a dormant part of my brain lit up. For years, my intellectual stimulation revolved around my business: the purchase of the right mix-and-blend tanks, proper concentrations of butterfat, problems associated with frozen distribution, and the ongoing war for supermarket shelf space. Every now and then we had a spirited discussion concerning the threats of E. coli bacteria.

Professor Perelman's presentation was a revelation. I was hooked in the first ten minutes.

Over the next two years, I volunteered for every Roundtable subcommittee and taskforce. The three meetings per year Dr. Lepley promised became three meetings per month. I helped develop a comprehensive school reform strategy that included higher standards and benchmarked, measurable results. Working with outside consultants and fellow Roundtable members, I helped to fashion an accountability system driven by strict rewards and penalties. I was a contributing author of our "World-

Class Schools" report, and I took a lead role in presenting our plan to the Governor and members of our state legislature.

I got so involved that in January 1990, I left the world of ice cream and became the Iowa Business Roundtable's first executive director. Now I had a platform from which to pontificate, and I did so with a vengeance. I was vocal, critical, and motivated.

Education groups expressed little interest in my views, but chambers of commerce and business organizations across the state were eager to hear my message. I crisscrossed the state dozens of times. I ate more rubber chicken than any candidate running for governor. I wrote Op-Ed pieces. I appeared on TV and radio. My speeches were cheered in every one of the ninety-nine counties between the Missouri and Mississippi rivers. I delivered the business gospel of school reform, and I received an ovation at every stop. My life was good.

In all those months, however, I did not manage to make or inspire a single improvement in Iowa's schools. My principal accomplishment in the public education arena was the complete alienation of the education establishment. The people who were needed to effect real change viewed me as a menace. Little Captain Kirks inside their heads would yell "Shields! Shields!" whenever I walked into the room.

In retrospect, I was the perfect double threat: ignorant and arrogant. I knew nothing about teaching or managing a school, but I was sure I had the answers.

Twenty years have passed since that grand initial tour, and much has changed. I have visited hundreds of schools. I have stood on hundreds of stages and talked with tens of thousands of teachers, administrators, board members, support staff, foundation members, business and community leaders, and parent groups. I've served on various education committees and sat on the boards of the federal educational laboratory in Chicago and the National PTA. Of course, none of this makes me an educator, but I am pleased and proud to be called a friend.

I would love to say that my transition from critic to ally was speedy, but that would not be true. Human beings rarely abandon their stated position simply because they are presented with a contradictory set of facts. (Ask anyone who is married.) I started out convinced that I was right, and my peers and politicians at every level of government supported my views. I was a prisoner of my prejudices. My transformation took years.

There were, however, a few seminal moments—moments when courageous educators actually listened to my message and took the time out of their grueling schedule to set me straight. They may have been furious with me, they may have been biting their tongues until they were bloody, but they were never mean or threatening. (Okay, once I was left alone with a scary group of UniServ directors intent on helping me see the error of my ways, but that's another story.) Patiently and methodically, teachers, administrators, and board members across the country endeavored to show me what it was like to live and work inside their world. They helped me see that my opinions, like those of most people who have little contact with schools, were based on selective memories, misinformation, half-truths, and outright lies. Their stories provided a powerful antidote to my negativity. Their efforts to engage me changed my life and opened me to a world of new understanding. I am in their debt.

The first of these transformative encounters occurred on a snowy day in January 1991. When it was over, my conviction that we needed to run our schools like a business was gone.

Chapter 2

The Blueberry Story

My heart stood still...

Antoine (Fats Domino) Dominique

During my first year on the road, not once was I asked to speak to an education audience. It was no surprise. The vast majority of Iowa's educators objected to the threatening tone of the Roundtable's message, and many were openly hostile toward me as its messenger. I was, therefore, amazed and very pleased when I received an invitation to speak to the district staff in a small town in western Iowa.

"Finally," I exclaimed, "someone on the inside is going to listen and adopt our agenda."

In retrospect it is clear that the superintendent had other plans. He either a) hated his staff and wanted to punish them for an hour, or b) wanted everyone to get a better view of the enemy. The smart bet is b.

I arrived on the appointed day and was taken to the high school auditorium. I sat on the stage alone and watched the seats slowly fill—back to front—with teachers, principals, bus drivers, secretaries, custodians, food service workers, and paraprofessionals. Unbeknownst to me, their local paper had recently reprinted one of my negative Op-Ed pieces, so everyone was angry before they even entered the room. In addition, this was their only in-service (professional development) program for three months, and instead of hearing something useful about curriculum, instruction, or technology, they were forced to waste their precious time listening to me: a bully in a suit from the city. They were livid.

At 8:15 a.m. sharp, the principal of the school stepped to the podium and said, "Good morning." This elicited a feeble reply. Normally in this situation, he would have repeated himself with gusto to get their attention and provoke enthusiasm. On this morning, however, he let it pass without comment. "This is Mr. Vollmer," he said without looking at me. "He's here from Des Moines representing a business group that's been studying our problems, and he's come to tell us what we are doing wrong." He then turned, and left the stage. I swear, you could have cut the animosity with a knife.

I didn't care. I stepped to the podium undaunted. After months of practice, I had it down.

"This is a talk about change," I proclaimed.

This sentence was immediately followed by a pronounced rustling noise. Teachers began to rifle their files, pull out notebooks, and openly grade papers in front of me. Some shared notes with their neighbors. Some turned their backs on me to talk with people behind them. Some read magazines—in the front row! I was up there giving my speech and there was a roar in the room.

But they were not going to bully me! I decided to up the ante. My tone became more strident, my rhetoric more negative.

"The status quo is killing us. We are not getting the workers that we need, and we're falling behind our competitors. There has been enough tinkering at the edges and enough excuses. You have to look to the world of business to solve your problems. Business leaders invented Total Quality Management. We understand continuous improvement. Just-in-time-delivery! Zero defects! We know that to produce real quality it is necessary to introduce benchmarked standards and meaningful accountability attached to serious rewards and penalties. I have to tell you, I wouldn't be in business very long if I ran my company the way you run your schools."

After about fifteen minutes, no one was grading papers. All pens and pencils were down, and they were glaring at me through clenched teeth.

Thirty minutes later, I concluded my talk with a flourish and waited for the response. Forget applause. The room was dead silent, and I have to admit that I was a tad intimidated.

As I turned to exit the stage, I saw the superintendent standing in the wings. He had no intention of coming out, but he was waving me back and whispering "Q and A. Q and A."

It was then that I remembered that I had promised to do a question and answer session after my talk. Slowly I turned, and walked back to the podium.

As soon as I got there, a woman's hand shot up, right in the middle of the room. I looked at her. She appeared to be pleasant—a nice looking woman of a certain age. I thought, "She'll be polite. I'll start with her." I found out later that she was a razor-tongued, high school English teacher with twenty seven years on the job who had been laying in the bushes for me for about an hour.

She began just as nice as you please. "Mr. Vollmer," she said, "we're told you make good ice cream."

I was insufferably smug in those days. "Yes, ma'am," I replied. "Best ice cream in America."

"How nice," she said. "Is it rich and smooth?"

"Seventeen percent butterfat. Low overrun, which means minimal air content. Smooth and creamy. You would love it."

"Yes," she continued without a beat. "I assume, sir, that you use nothing but Grade A ingredients. Your flavorings, nuts and berries…"

"Excuse me, ma'am," I interrupted. "At The Great Midwestern

Ice Cream Company, our specification to our suppliers is triple A."

A little smile flashed across her face that I did not understand at the time. I never saw the next line coming.

"Mr. Vollmer," she said, leaning forward with a predatory look that raised the hair on my neck, "when you are in your factory, standing on the receiving dock, and you see a shipment of blueberries arrive, and those blueberries do not meet your triple A standards, what do you do?"

In the silence of that room, you could hear the trap snap. I was dead meat.

Nobody moved. All eyes were fixed. I was one moment away from being eviscerated, but I wasn't going to lie.

"I send them back."

Wham!

She sprang to her feet, pointed her finger at my face and said, "That's right! You send them back. We can never send back the blueberries *our* suppliers send us. We take them big, small, rich, poor, hungry, abused, confident, curious, homeless, frightened, rude, creative, violent, and brilliant. We take them of every race, religion, and ethnic background. We take them with head lice, ADHD, and advanced asthma. We take them with juvenile rheumatoid arthritis, English as their second language, and who knows how much lead in their veins. We take them all, Mr. Vollmer! Every one! And *that's* why it's not a business. It's school!"

Well.

I would have gotten the point. But before I could respond, all 290 of them jumped to their feet in an explosion of clapping and whistling, yelling, "Yeah! Blueberries! Blueberries!"

My world would never be quite the same.

My friends in business have argued since that she painted with a broad brush. Sure she did—she had ninety seconds. I have, however, visited hundreds of schools since that day and her analogy remains apt. Unlike most businesses, public schools have no control over the quality of their "raw material." They take what the parents send, and, sadly, more damaged blueberries arrive every day. High levels of student turnover exacerbate the problem of quality control. Kids with markedly different backgrounds come and go at random throughout the year. This constant churning undermines the validity of any accountability system that tracks the progress of groups as opposed to individuals.

The business model has other flaws. I hear all sorts of righteous comments from businesspeople that our schools need to serve the customer, but no one can even agree on who the customers are. Candidates include students, parents, grandparents, business owners, corporate executives, human resource directors, deans of admission, and the entire taxpaying public, seventy percent of whom have no kids in school. And none of these parties can agree on what they want as a finished product except in the broadest terms. Politicians and bureaucrats are left to define and endlessly redefine what children should know and when they should know it; they do this while being manipulated by a howling horde of organized, aggressive, well-funded special interest groups. Many of these groups have agendas that are directly at odds with the best interests of kids, and all of them know exactly how our schools should operate. They wage their campaigns from classrooms and principals' offices to the halls of Congress. As a young man, I worked for a Washington, D.C. law firm that represented major airlines, one of America's most highly regulated industries, but I never saw anything like the lobbying brawl that surrounds our public schools.

Finally, there is the bizarre method of funding. When it comes to generating a reliable revenue stream, public schools are entirely dependent upon the mood of the general public as reflected in the vagaries of local, state, and federal politics. Superintendents and their boards often take months to craft reasoned and reasonable proposals for needed funds only to watch in horror on election night as they are defeated by a "citizens" antitax group animated by a grudge against the football coach. Add to the mix a governing process that sometimes produces board members who are specifically elected to retard progress, and you have a "business" that would send America's top CEOs screaming into the night.

There is no doubt that we can successfully graft certain business practices onto the unique culture of public schools. And we should. Aspects of the Quality Movement have much to offer, especially those that promote learning communities, feedback loops, long-term commitments to excellence, and quality professional development. But the more I learned about the system, the more certain I became that the blueberry lady was right.

Years have passed since that snowy day when one teacher stood up and engaged the enemy. I towered over her on that stage, strong, determined, and articulate. (Suspend your disbelief.) I had the referent power of the entire political and business establishment at my back. That woman could have fumed in silence. She could have simply cursed my skinny butt all the way back to her room. Instead, she grit her teeth and pushed back. She hit the wall of negativity head on. She challenged my simplistic, self-serving beliefs armed with nothing more than the knowledge born of her daily experience—in other words, the truth—and, in doing so, she forced me to rethink my views.

I drove from the parking lot feeling a bit unsettled and abused.

As I reflected on my visit over the next few days, however, I began to regroup. My core belief was that our schools were not delivering the required results, and something needed to change. This belief had not been challenged. In fact, nothing the teacher said suggested that she and the others had any incentive to work hard to change the status quo. She just resented an outsider pushing reforms based on false assumptions. I may have been a jerk, my business prescription may have been simplistic, but I had no reason to doubt my diagnosis: the people were the problem. Within weeks, I would be forced to rethink that, too.

Chapter 3

An Aide for a Day

*It ain't so much the things we don't know that gets us
into trouble. It's the things we know that just ain't so.*

Artemus Ward

Human beings form assumptions to make sense of the
world. We construct our assumptions from facts, opinions,
memories, and intuition. Not all of our assumptions are correct.
Some are based on false information. Others are shaped by our
prejudices and beliefs. Over time, erroneous assumptions can co-
alesce to create cognitive illusions—distorted perceptions of reality. We accept things as facts that just ain't so. Certain Eastern
philosophies hold that the entire universe is a cognitive illusion—
it simply does not exist—but that is beyond my ken. My mortgage
seems real enough to me.

Our illusions are dangerous because they subvert our power
of reasoning. They warp our worldview without our knowing it.
They are difficult to recognize and therefore hard to change. We
can make little progress toward comprehending the truth until
they are identified and corrected.

My assumption regarding the problem with our schools is a
perfect example. It grew out of simplistic media coverage, political spin, my belief in the power of the free market, my suspicions about the efficiency of public institutions, and my near total

lack of understanding of what actually goes on in our schools. All these combined to convince me that our educators were the primary obstacles to reform. None of them were exposed to the competitive forces of the marketplace. Teachers sat in their pension-feathered nests cloaked in tenure. Administrators shielded themselves behind a monopolistic bureaucracy where they used government rules and regulations as excuses for inertia. The only way we were going to get world-class schools was to hold these people accountable and force them to improve. I believed it all, and I said it all.

It's likely that I would be saying it still but for some savvy people who figured out a way to break the spell. Their strategy was simple. Don't argue. Just let the big shot see for himself what it's really like inside our world.

Within a week of my blueberry experience, invitations to visit other districts arrived. I guess the word got out among superintendents: "Invite Jamie. Your staff will maul him."

In the months that followed, I took tours of school buildings. I sat through board meetings that extended into the wee hours of the morning. I watched a principal and members of his staff fill out a mountain of forms required by the state and federal governments. I attended faculty meetings, and in doing so, I learned why teachers say that they hope to die in one: the transition from stuporous boredom to death would be so subtle that they would hardly notice.

Every visit was instructive and influenced my views. But the crushing blow came from a superintendent in a river town on the Mississippi who invited me to spend an entire day working in his schools.

The day started with my doing bus duty at the elementary school, after which I was escorted to a third grade classroom to be a teacher's aide. I spent the morning working with twenty-seven eight-year-olds, including one severe asthmatic, one confirmed victim of sexual assault, four identified with ADHD, two requiring speech therapy, and one sweet girl with cerebral palsy who required a full inclusion team. The kids were creative, curious, precocious, eager, helpful, and, above all, energetic. Sitting was not on the agenda.

At noon I was taken to lunch. Not at a restaurant downtown, which would have been the sociable thing to do, and not in the cafeteria, which is a harrowing experience that I've had many times since. No. They took me to the teachers' lounge. For the uninitiated, this is not a pretty sight: a bunch of harried grownups using twenty minutes to inhale food, gossip, and cut out paper pumpkins, turkeys, wreaths, hearts, or shamrocks depending on the season. Not fine dining. I managed to eat my sandwich and squeeze in a quick trip to the men's room—my only one of the day—before running to be a playground monitor.

After lunch, I was taken to a middle school to work with eighth graders. It was a warm Friday afternoon in May. Most of the kids were thirteen. Some looked like babies. Some, especially the young woman wearing a halter top and green eye shadow, looked twenty-three. When I was introduced as a temporary aide, they looked through me as though I didn't exist. I have since determined that no one is qualified to criticize public schools unless he or she has been locked in a room with a similar group. It is the litmus test of credibility. There was an interesting smell in that room.

When the final bell rang, I nearly wept with joy.

I was spared having to do any of the after-school chores that are routine for most teachers; I was not asked to grade papers, prepare lessons, or supervise extracurricular activities. Instead, the superintendent took me to his office to meet with his board president and the president of the local teachers' association.

I was exhausted. I had not spent an entire day on my feet in years. My shoulders ached. My shins hurt. My hair was sticking out on the sides—I looked like Linus after a long day without his blanket. I would have offered my firstborn for Advil and caffeine, and I wouldn't have turned down a beaker full of gin.

In retrospect I realize that my hosts had taken a risk by inviting me to come. They gambled that anyone who worked in a school even for one day could not fail to be awed by the rigors of the job or moved by the effort and dedication of the people who teach. This was their moment of truth.

I broke the silence. "This is hard, isn't it?"

"Yes," they said in unison. I got the impression they suppressed a round of high fives.

"I have one question," I said. "Is what I saw and what I experienced typical?"

"It is," the superintendent said, "for ninety percent of the staff, ninety percent of the time." The others nodded.

I took them at their word, and let the weight of their answer settle in. As it did, I felt a shift in my psyche, deep down where my cognitive illusions reside.

Admittedly, the day was harder for me because I was unprepared, and the eighth grade ordeal was just plain cruel, but there was no way that anyone could walk away from this experience and argue that the educators were indifferent. Everyone I saw was working hard. Really hard.

Once again, I drove away from a school faced with the strong possibility that I'd been wrong. (I was getting tired of that.) I saw no teachers and administrators who were lazy or apathetic. I had no way of knowing if they were employing state-of-the-art practices in their classrooms, but they were smart, dedicated, and professional—intently focused on helping their students succeed. I was, however, still faced with the fact that something was wrong. Dramatic changes were transforming our society, especially the economy, and our schools were becoming dangerously out of sync with the needs of the time.

What struck me as I reviewed the day was that much of what I had experienced seemed remarkably familiar. The schools looked the same and felt the same as they had years before. The movement of students and the way they were grouped were reminiscent, if not identical, to the patterns I had known in the 1950s and 1960s—patterns established well before World War II. In many ways, I felt as though I had entered a time warp.

I continued to accept invitations to visit other districts, but I began to listen more than speak. Once it became clear that I was honestly trying to figure things out, teachers, administrators, and board members lowered their defensive shields and began to share their experiences. Soon, I had too much evidence contradicting my assumptions to sweep under the rug. My illusion gave way, and an unnerving question began to form in its place. What if we do not have a people problem? What if the problem is deep in the system?

This thought was sobering on two counts. First, it suggested that thirty years of reform initiatives aimed at changing behavior via performance incentives, teacher-proof materials, site-based councils, raised standards, wall-to-wall testing, and school take-overs were missing the core problem, which would explain a lot. Second, and much more vexing, fixing a people problem was a formidable challenge, but fixing a massive, heavily regulated, culturally entrenched system was a task that was harder by a factor of a thousand. I had no more than a layman's understanding of the magnitude of this problem, but the complexity made my head spin. It was time to find out if I had finally glimpsed the scary truth.

Chapter 4

The Ever-Increasing Burden

*A man should look for what is, and not
for what he thinks should be.*

Albert Einstein

T he next two years were a time of intense study. I had to
learn a new language, new concepts, the basic history of
public education, the rudiments of school funding and finance,
and a whole lot more about what it was like to work in a school.
There were times when it was like being back in law school, minus
the all-nighters and eight hour exams.

So many people helped me along the way.

I was invited to join a Midwest study group called the School
Transformation Council. It was comprised of representatives from
various state agencies who had been thinking for years about how
to increase student success. They were very smart, and their discussions were both practical and provocative.

At the same time, as director of the Business Roundtable, I
was chosen to serve on the board of the North Central Regional
Education Laboratory, one of seven R&D Labs created by the U.S.
Department of Education to provide states with proven classroom
practices and technical assistance. My position gave me direct access to a national network of expert practitioners and theorists
and a terrific library of resources.

Between the two groups, I was introduced to the thinking of people representing every point of the political spectrum: from Ernest Boyer and David Berliner, to E.D. Hirsch and David Kearns; from Deborah Meier and Phillip Schlecty, to Diane Ravitch and Chester Finn. Books, reports, journals, and articles lay in great piles on the floor surrounding my desk.

I had no background in education, which made for a steep learning curve, but it turned out to be a huge asset. I had no vested interest in any program. My ego was not attached to a particular school of thought. I had little allegiance to the sacred cows of the status quo. I approached each topic from a business perspective, which engendered a predisposition to focus on outcomes. My legal training helped me isolate the issues and assemble the facts.

I began by looking more closely at the children we were trying to teach. Like so many outsiders, I had little understanding of just how much America's public school students had changed. I was shocked to learn that twenty-two percent lived in poverty, the highest rate in the industrialized world. These children suffered from high rates of physical and mental health problems. Many displayed the effects of lead poisoning, and hundreds of thousands had no permanent address. I knew we had become more diverse as a nation, but I had no idea that forty percent of all students were minorities, many part of the largest wave of immigrants in our history. These kids had little education in the countries they left, and most spoke no English when they arrived. The special education legislation of the 1970s had added to the school rolls millions of kids with special needs, some requiring intense intervention. Weak, incompetent parenting was forcing teachers and administrators to devote time and energy to rude and unruly children—children who were socialized by watching thousands of hours of television, children who were manipulated by a predatory commercial culture that skewed their values and instilled a dangerously overdeveloped sense of entitlement. The students of my youth had morphed into a most difficult population to teach.

My growing understanding of these students led me to consider how much we had added to the curriculum since the first schools were established. In order to keep track of the additions, I was forced to develop a decade-by-decade list of all the academic, social, and health responsibilities that have been heaped upon our schools. I called my work product the "Increasing Burden On America's Schools," but it has since become known across the country simply as Vollmer's List.

I found that for a long time we added nothing. The Massachusetts Puritans who started it all assumed that families and churches bore the major responsibility for raising a child. Their mandate to the teachers was simple: teach basic reading, some writing and rudimentary math skills, and cultivate values that serve a democratic society (some history and civics were implied). In the mid 1700s, Benjamin Franklin added some science and geography, but the curriculum remained focused for 260 years.

At the beginning of the twentieth century, however, politicians, academics, members of the clergy, and business leaders saw public schools as a logical site for the assimilation of immigrants and the social engineering of the citizens—and workers—of the new industrial age. They began to expand the curriculum and assign additional duties. That trend has accelerated ever since.

From **1900 to 1910**, we shifted to the school responsibilities related to:

- Nutrition
- Immunization
- Health (Activities in the health arena multiply every year.)

From **1910 to 1930,** we added:

- Physical education (including organized athletics)
- The Practical Arts/Domestic Science/Home economics (including

sewing and cooking)
- Vocational education (including industrial and agricultural education)
- Mandated school transportation

In the **1940s,** we added:

- Business education (including typing, shorthand, and bookkeeping)
- Art and music
- Speech and drama
- Half-day kindergarten
- School lunch programs (We take this for granted today, but it was a huge step to shift to the schools the job of feeding America's children one third of their daily meals.)

In the **1950s,** we added:

- Expanded science and math education
- Safety education
- Driver's education
- Expanded music and art education
- Stronger foreign language requirements
- Sex education (Topics continue to escalate.)

In the **1960s**, we added:

- Advanced Placement programs
- Head Start
- Title I
- Adult education
- Consumer education (resources, rights and responsibilities)
- Career education (options and entry level skill requirements)
- Peace, leisure, and recreation education [Loved those sixties.]

In the **1970s**, the breakup of the American family accelerated, and we added:

- Drug and alcohol abuse education
- Parenting education (techniques and tools for healthy parenting)
- Behavior adjustment classes (including classroom and communication skills)

- Character education
- Special education (mandated by federal government)
- Title IX programs (greatly expanded athletic programs for girls)
- Environmental education
- Women's studies
- African-American heritage education
- School breakfast programs (Now some schools feed America's children two-thirds of their daily meals throughout the school year and all summer. Sadly, these are the only decent meals some children receive.)

In the **1980s**, the floodgates opened, and we added:

- Keyboarding and computer education
- Global education
- Multicultural/Ethnic education
- Nonsexist education
- English-as-a-second-language and bilingual education
- Teen pregnancy awareness
- Hispanic heritage education
- Early childhood education
- Jump Start, Early Start, Even Start, and Prime Start
- Full-day kindergarten
- Preschool programs for children at risk
- After-school programs for children of working parents
- Alternative education in all its forms
- Stranger/danger education
- Antismoking education
- Sexual abuse prevention education
- Expanded health and psychological services
- Child abuse monitoring (a legal requirement for all teachers)

In the **1990s**, we added:

- Conflict resolution and peer mediation
- HIV/AIDS education
- CPR training
- Death education

- America 2000 initiatives (Republican)
- Inclusion
- Expanded computer and internet education
- Distance learning
- Tech Prep and School to Work programs
- Technical Adequacy Assessment
- Post-secondary enrollment options
- Concurrent enrollment options
- Goals 2000 initiatives (Democrat)
- Expanded Talented and Gifted opportunities
- At risk and dropout prevention
- Homeless education (including causes and effects on children)
- Gang education (urban centers)
- Service learning
- Bus safety, bicycle safety, gun safety, and water safety education

In the first decade of the twenty-first century, we have added:

- No Child Left Behind (Republican)
- Bully prevention
- Anti-harassment policies (gender, race, religion, or national origin)
- Expanded early childcare and wrap around programs
- Elevator and escalator safety instruction
- Body Mass Index evaluation (obesity monitoring)
- Organ donor education and awareness programs
- Personal financial literacy
- Entrepreneurial and innovation skills development
- Media literacy development
- Contextual learning skill development
- Health and wellness programs
- Race to the Top (Democrat)

This list does not include the addition of multiple, specialized topics within each of the traditional subjects. It also does not include the explosion of standardized testing and test prep activities, or any of the onerous reporting requirements imposed by

the federal government, such as four-year adjusted cohort graduation rates, parental notification of optional supplemental services, comprehensive restructuring plans, and reports of Adequate
Yearly Progress.

It's a ponderous list.[1]

Each item has merit, and all have their ardent supporters, but
the truth is that we have added these responsibilities without adding a single minute to the school calendar in six decades. No generation of teachers and administrators in the history of the world
has been told to fulfill this mandate: not just teach children, but
raise them!

As shocking as the list was, no discovery about our schools was
more surprising or had a greater impact on my thinking than the
amazing record of their success.

By this point I knew that most teachers and administrators
were working hard at one of the most difficult and complex jobs
in the world: cultivating human intelligence. In classroom after
classroom, I saw teachers striving to introduce the right stimuli
at the right time and reinforce each step of student progress in
supportive learning environments that they had created. What
I did not know, however, was that they were making great progress. Contrary to public opinion, most of the traditional indicators of student success were not down, but up. Since the 1960s,
enrollment and attendance were up. The average number of
courses taken in high school and their degree of difficulty were
up, as were the number of Advanced Placement courses taken and
passed. Graduation rates—a tricky statistic to accurately measure
in a mobile society—were steady to slightly up. The number of
graduates going on to college and the percentage of those who
graduated with a degree were up—remarkably so for minorities.
Alarmist headlines notwithstanding, an honest analysis of standardized test results showed that disaggregated scores on the

---

[1] Copies available in poster form at www.jamievollmer.com.

NAEP, SAT, and ACT were improving, albeit slowly. It was true that the average scores—what the media reported—were down, but this was because more kids from the middle and the bottom of the class were taking the tests, a statistical phenomenon known as Simpson's Paradox. Even in the international arena, where public schools are much maligned, contrary to everything I had read and heard (and said), America's children were performing at high levels. Once again, the achievement was not seen in the average. To reach this conclusion it was necessary to parse the numbers and consider differences in the courses that were taken and the relative ages and socioeconomic status of test-takers.[2] But when apples were honestly compared to apples, we had, in fact, more students performing at the highest level on the TIMMS and PISA assessments than any of our international competitors.

All things considered, the record showed that every year since the 1983 release of *A Nation at Risk*, the people working in the vast majority of public schools had raised student achievement. Unfortunately, the record also showed that every year, America's students fell further behind; the gap grew between what our kids knew and what they needed to know to succeed in a post-industrial society.

For me, this was the final blow. I was increasingly overwhelmed with evidence that made my acceptance of the people problem harder to defend, but this made it impossible.

There was nothing wrong with demanding diligence and accountability; everyone can, and must, improve, and most teachers and administrators I'd met were open to practical ideas that would further student achievement. But we were never going to close the knowledge gap by continuing to assume that the system was sound and forcing an already overburdened workforce to work harder, not just over the short run, but forever. I understood

---

[2] From country to country, for example, there can be as much as a three-year difference in the average age of high school seniors, from 17 to 20.

enough about the Quality Movement to know that the top-down imposition of accountability measures that emphasized extrinsic rewards and sanctions, ridicule, and threats of job loss was not the path to excellence. Even if the strategy increased productivity by fifteen percent—a sensational outcome in any organization—it still would not be enough to deliver the graduates we required. We had to make a quantum leap, not incremental progress. Ideally, we had to unfold the full creative potential of every child. At a bare minimum, we had to prepare almost every child for advanced learning in some post-secondary program, a feat that no society in the history of the world had even contemplated, let alone accomplished. A strategy of blaming, demonizing, and intimidating educators was not only futile, it was counterproductive. Something had to change.

Months passed, and I reached the point where my brain was supersaturated with statistics, facts, opinions, theories, and questions. The few answers I managed to comprehend were seen through a glass darkly, at best.

And then, out of the blue, I read something that caused everything to fall into place.

Ironically, after all my exposure to the research and theory of twentieth century educators, my catastrophic moment was triggered by a single sentence written in the eighteenth century by one of our Founding Fathers. I read his words, and instantly I knew that my suspicions were correct. There was a major flaw in the design of the system, and I knew what it was.

PART II

Why Our Schools Need to Change

Chapter 5

The Flaw in the System

Twenty years of schoolin' and they put you on the day shift.

Bob Dylan

A merica's schools were not designed to teach all children to high levels. They were designed to select and sort young people into two groups: a small handful of thinkers and a great mass of doers according to the workplace needs of an agro-industrial society. As long as this design remains in tact, millions of teachers and administrators will struggle to deliver outcomes that the system was never designed to produce.

It started with Jefferson.

There were schools in the colonies as early as 1635, but, as Governor of Virginia, Thomas Jefferson created the first statewide, two-track system of public education in 1780. Jefferson considered it imperative that all children (white boys) be educated at the public's expense, regardless of wealth or birth. He argued that each child should be educated "well enough" to a) transact his business, and b) effectively participate in the civic life of his community. At no point, however, did Jefferson contend that every child should receive the *same* education. He believed in a "natural aristocracy." Borrowing from the writings of John Locke, he saw Americans divided into two distinct classes, the "laboring" and the "learned," and he designed an education process to prepare young people to assume their respective roles.

His approach to grooming a leadership elite was simple. In *Notes on the state of Virginia, 1781-2,* he proposed a network of districts with a school within three miles of every home. Families could send their children to these schools for three years at no cost. At the end of each year, the primary school teachers were to:

> [C]huse the boy, of best genius in the school, of those whose parents are too poor to give them further education, and send him forward to one of the grammar schools.... Of the boys thus sent in any one year, trial is to be made at the grammar schools [in] one or two years, and the best genius of the whole selected, and continued six years, and the residue dismissed. By this means twenty of the best *geniusses will be raked from the rubbish* annually, and be instructed, at the public expence.... At the end of six years instruction, one half are to be discontinued ... and the other half, who are to be chosen for the superiority of their parts and disposition, are to be sent and continued three years in the study of such sciences as they shall chuse, at William and Mary college.... [Emphasis added.]

The teaching strategies were rudimentary. Children of varying ages worked together, usually in one room, progressing at their own pace through a curriculum dominated by memorizing words and poems. There was little writing or computation. Books and supplies were scarce. Discipline was harsh. Attendance was minimal.

It may sound dreary, but Jefferson's plan was a great leap forward on two counts. First, every eligible boy could now receive at least some basic education for free. Second, the young *geniusses* who managed to advance now had access to the education they needed to compete with children of position and wealth. The boys who were identified as "rubbish" ended their formal education and went to work. Girls had only one option: learn home-making from their mothers.

This raking process was tough on late bloomers, it made no accommodation for differing learning styles, and it offered nothing to minorities or those white children whose parents either could not or would not send them to school. But from society's perspective, the system worked. There was little need to cultivate more than a handful of geniuses. The economy was relatively simple. Most Americans lived on farms. Financial success was based on the ability of an individual or a business to arrange the right combination of the following factors in a productive relationship:

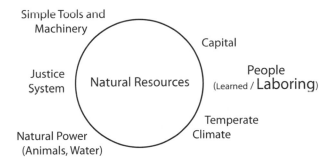

Figure 1. Core competitive advantages of the Agricultural Age.

This was the competitive formula of the agricultural age, and Jefferson's selecting model was perfectly suited to supply the requisite number of learners and laborers in proper proportion. By 1880, replicas of his model were operating in all thirty-eight states.

The *chusing and raking* continued largely unchanged until the end of the nineteenth century, when the first national wave of reform began. It was triggered by an unprecedented social and economic transformation. By the time William McKinley was re-elected President in 1900 (on the catchy slogan, "Four More Years of the Full Dinner Pail"), the population of the United States and its territories had grown to fifty million people—up from two million when Jefferson served—and the second industrial revolution was in high gear. The pace of change was slow by today's standards, but every aspect of society was being remade, and none more than the economy. Steam engines, electrification, and applied science fundamentally changed the rules of competition. The economic formula that had existed for thousands of years was recast. New elements were added, and the relative importance of the traditional factors shifted:

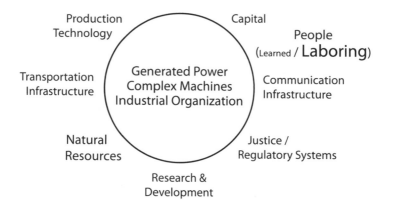

Figure 2. Core competitive advantages of the Industrial Age.

Businessmen who understood the new rules built immense fortunes by concentrating capital and labor around complex and expensive machines. These "industrialists" systemized every aspect of production. Their factories replaced farms as the principal place of work.

Millions of rural Americans flocked to the cities where they joined millions of new European immigrants in hoping for greater comfort and security. They entered the regimented world of the assembly line where their actions were closely monitored and tightly controlled. They were paid to do what they were told—no more, no less—by foremen who used intimidation, profanity, and abuse to keep the line moving. Machines were designed to reduce employee discretion to a minimum. Thinking was reserved for the growing class of managers. Military style bureaucracies became the American way of work. The hours were long, conditions were brutal, but productivity soared and the economy grew at an extraordinary rate.

At the beginning of the industrial revolution, public schools experienced little change. Instead of working on the family farm, young children followed their parents into the factories, mines, and mills. But in the first decades of the twentieth century, changes in social policy, particularly child labor laws, brought millions of new students into the schools and kept them there for longer periods of time. The average public elementary school quickly doubled and tripled in size. High school enrollment, long considered a luxury, also exploded as it became clear to business leaders and policymakers that some secondary education for the laboring class would increase economic output. As the size and composition of the student population changed, reformers on the left and right began to call for a major overhaul of America's schools.

Social progressives, led by John Dewey, attacked the established design head-on; they wanted to abolish the selecting process altogether. In speeches, articles, and essays, they condemned rote learning and mindless, one-size-fits-all teaching. They endorsed "student-centered" methods of instruction with "experience-based" curricula; they saw public school as a place not only to teach the basics, but to mold the individual and promote social justice. Progressives had victories, but they were opposed and eventually overwhelmed by a coalition of "administrative reformers" who advanced a very different agenda.

These men, led by Charles Judd and Edward Thorndike, also complained bitterly about the quality of public schools, but they didn't want to replace the selecting process; they wanted to improve it. The economy had changed, but the learner-to-laborer ratio had not. The industrial workplace demanded marginally higher levels of literacy, but it was still comprised of a small handful of thinkers and a great mass of doers. Administrative reformers saw school as the logical place to sort the two groups, and they wanted to expedite the process. They sought to systematize and consolidate America's loose network of "common schools" so that they could be more centrally controlled and professionally managed. Unfolding the full potential of every child was neither necessary nor practical, and it was definitely not on their agenda.

This movement was epitomized by a panel of university presidents called the Committee of Ten. The group came together in 1891 to focus on "the general subject of uniformity in school programmes, and on requirements for admission to college." Their seminal report, issued a year later, firmly established not only which subjects should be taught, but when they should be taught, in what order, and for how long. The Committee, like Jefferson, divided America's students into two groups: the "academic" (those going on to college) and the "terminal" (everyone else). Unlike Jefferson, however, whose learner and laborer categories were implied in the selecting process, the Committee's labels were explicit; they became part of the language of school. And once applied to a child, the label was exposed for every classmate, every teacher, and every parent to see.

A decade later, the Carnegie Foundation for Advancement of Teaching took the formalizing process a step further; they standardized the school day—down to the minute—including the exact time of each class and the number of "Carnegie Units" awarded for each subject. As we shall see, it was this rigid structuring of time that cast the selecting process in stone.

By the 1930s, the concept of schools-as-factories had become a powerful organizing metaphor. Public schools adopted the architecture, language, and methods of the factory. Fredrick Taylor's theories of "scientific management" swept the system—one of the first examples of the "people problem" approach to school reform. Corporate-style boards of education were created to manage "rationalized accounting systems" and "standardized operating procedures." Administrators, especially superintendents, were charged with the dual responsibilities of raising educational standards while increasing organizational efficiency. Financial considerations became entwined with educational considerations. As in the factory, worker discretion and control were discouraged as "teaching machines" and "teacher proof" instructional materials flooded the schools.

To enhance the selecting process, the curriculum was broken into discrete, decontextualized units of knowledge taught by teachers who were given no time or incentive to collaborate. America's students were treated as raw material sliding along an assembly line at the sound of a bell. They were sequestered from the real world and isolated in classrooms where a tolerance for boredom was cultivated. They were "drilled," "polished," and "molded" in settings where their behavior could be predicted and controlled. They were "tracked" and prepared to "adjust to life" according to their anticipated status as thinkers or doers in the two-tiered world of work. Unlike their agrarian age predecessors who worked in multi-age classrooms and moved through the curriculum at their own pace, picking up in the fall where they left off in the spring, the students in the factory model were grouped strictly according to age, tied to the clock, and expected to progress with their group. This expectation of "graduating with your class" introduced the concept of failure into the education process along with its debilitating social stigma.

All these reforms streamlined the system, but nothing advanced the cause of sorting efficiency as much as the introduction of the standardized test.

Alfred Binet, a French psychologist specializing in child development, created the first intelligence test in 1905. He intended that his diagnostic test be used narrowly to identify a student's strengths and weaknesses *specifically related* to schoolwork. And he stressed that the test could only be used on children with comparable backgrounds. Administrative reformers, however, saw the test in broader terms. They perceived its potential not as a diagnostic tool, but as a way to establish an individual's overall level of intelligence. (It's interesting to note that the earliest promoters were also champions of eugenics.) Their cause was greatly advanced in 1917, when Harvard psychologist Robert Yerkes devised a multiple-choice form of Binet's test that could be administered on a mass scale. It was originally designed to assist military recruitment in World War I, but American educators, and the American public, embraced his creation as a way to quickly identify who was smart and who was not on the basis of a normalized box score. An orgy of standardized, norm-referenced, machine-scored testing soon engulfed the nation's schools. The tests were administered as early as the third grade to channel students into curricular tracks and, consequently, into the world of work. In an historical blink, the results that Binet used to forecast a child's likely performance in school, now announced to the world what his or her potential was *in life*.

By the end of World War II, the industrialization of education was complete. As in Jefferson's day, the new and improved selecting process left much to be desired. Racial inequality was rampant. There was tremendous inequality of access, programs, materials, and facilities. Student tracking was strongly influenced by a child's socioeconomic status. The rigid adherence to schedules, the narrow, decontextualized curriculum, and the one-size-fits-all approach to teaching and testing resulted in a tremendous waste of human potential. Progressive descendants of Dewey continually assailed the system's authoritarian methods and disregard for the whole child. But, to borrow a phrase from the humorist

Al Capp, "What's good for General Bullmoose, is good for the U.S.A." America had become a superpower. Our workforce, combined with our capital, production techniques, technology, and equipment was the envy of the world. America's political leaders created social safety nets to minimize the economic instabilities inherent in capitalism, and unions fought to ensure that workers benefited from the unprecedented rise in productivity.

Businesses grew. People got jobs. Millions caught the American Dream. The selecting system worked. As long as our schools delivered the learned and laboring classes in proper proportion, and as long as productivity and standards of living continued to soar, there was no practical reason to change.

And there would be none now, except for one momentous and inescapable fact: we are no longer getting what we need. The symbiotic relationship between our schools and the workplace is broken. Every year, our schools teach more children in more subjects to higher levels, and, every year, millions leave school with nowhere to go. In an ironic twist, the human capital needs of the American economy that gave rise to the selecting system and justified its existence for centuries, now provide irrefutable reasons to end it.

Chapter 6

The New Competitive Equation

The wise one knows what time it is.

Zen Proverb

Once again, American society is being completely transformed, this time at the speed of light. The industrial age is being replaced by a post-industrial "knowledge age." Communism has failed. Capitalism is spreading across the world like a prairie fire with telecommunications acting as an accelerant. Separating the geniuses from the rubbish for an industrial workplace is not what we need.

Americans find themselves in a brutally competitive global market where our traditional competitive advantages are being marginalized, stolen, or sold. Our temperate climate, arable land, and abundant natural resources—the sources of our prosperity for centuries—no longer drive the economy. Even in Iowa, where my house sits surrounded by row crops for as far as the eye can see, less than ten percent of the people work in agriculture. American scientists and inventors lead the world in the number of patents awarded annually, but their breakthrough technologies are quickly acquired, disassembled, and reengineered abroad, often stripped of intellectual property rights. Our workers, once the envy of the world, are now challenged by an increasingly literate global labor force comprised of people who are hungry, eager, and willing to work for a fraction of the American wage. American capital pours across international boundaries seeking opportunities promising the highest rate of return.

Smart companies have adapted to this new reality. The best have become the world's richest corporations, and yet they control none of the traditional sources of wealth. They control knowledge. Their employees learn and apply what they have learned faster than their competition. Their CEOs understand that highly educated and skilled people are their key competitive advantage. To maximize this advantage, they place their employees in the center of a rewarding, supportive environment that nourishes the growth of creative intelligence, and they arrange all the traditional factors of production to revolve around this expanding core of knowledge. By organizing their companies in this way, the best managers have devised a new competitive equation—the winning formula of the knowledge age:

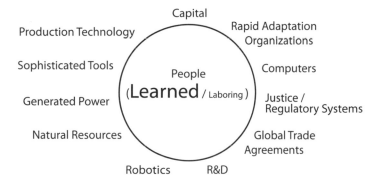

Figure 3. Core competitive advantage of the Knowledge Age.

What's most extraordinary about the new equation—and most alarming from the perspective of our schools—is that the "learned-to-laboring" ratio has been reversed. Not just changed. Reversed. Everywhere, lines are being blurred between the thinkers and doers. This reversal has never happened before in the history of humankind, and its effects are seen across all sectors of the economy.

In the established industrial sector, workers who once needed little more than manual dexterity and mechanical aptitude now work in settings where symbols and keyboards have replaced hammers and wrenches. Frontline workers increasingly function in self-directed, multi-ethnic teams where they work to set goals, develop budgets, control quality, and solve problems. In the rapidly expanding office economy, which now employs forty-one percent of our workforce and accounts for most of the job growth, cumbersome top-down hierarchies have been replaced by flatter, flexible organizations that give all employees greater discretion and control. Low and mid-level workers routinely direct physical, monetary, and intellectual resources that were once the exclusive domain of upper management. Employees who were previously relegated to menial tasks now are daily called upon to add value, variety, and convenience to existing products and services. They must have the skills to acquire and interpret information culled from diverse sources presented in multiple formats.

No one knows with certainty where the economy is headed, and the hoopla over the need to teach job-specific skills in high school is overblown—there are too many unknowns. But it is abundantly clear that low-skill/high-wage jobs are gone. A strong back, a willingness to work, and a tolerance for tedium will no longer afford access to the American Dream. Income inequalities between learner and laborer are rising; the poorly educated have been marginalized. We have reached the point where a good education—once considered a luxury by many— has become a basic requirement for success.

Today, almost every child must graduate, and almost every graduate must be prepared to pursue some form of post-secondary degree or certificate. In a single generation, we have raised the bar from requiring universal student *attendance* to demanding universal student *achievement*. No generation of educators in the history of the world has been asked to accomplish this goal. As a nation, we have promoted quality education for centuries, but never once have we provided even a simple majority of America's youth with the kind of education that virtually all of them need today. No wonder so many teachers and administrators are exhausted by Thanksgiving. The deck is stacked against them. They are struggling to teach all children to high levels in a system purposely designed to teach only some. The whole thing would be a joke if the stakes were not so high.

Jefferson had it right. Our public schools must educate America's children well enough to thrive in the workplace and participate as responsible members of their communities. The system he proposed worked. It produced what we needed within an acceptable margin of error for a very long time. But America has changed, and what it means to be educated "well enough" has changed with it. The limitations of this system, which continues to operate within almost all our schools, public and private, have been painfully exposed. We will never get what we need as long as the selecting premise prevails.

We must do all we can to empower, encourage, and, when appropriate, push all of the people working within our schools to function at their highest level; after parents, no one and nothing play a more important role in ensuring a child's success than his or her teachers, not even socioeconomic status. But no matter how hard or smart our educators work, the internal logic of the selecting machine will frustrate their efforts, and our schools will continue to produce legions of children who are unprepared to succeed as adults. The system is the primary problem. Its roots stretch back seven hundred years to the High Middle Ages. It has been operating in America for over two hundred years. Its traditions run deep in our veins. But unless and until it's changed, we will never successfully meet the challenges of our time.

❧❧

I had come a long way in my understanding of the problems facing our schools. I had arrived at the first Roundtable meeting convinced that our schools needed to change, and after four years of intense study, observation, and direct experience I was more convinced than ever. The difference was that I now knew why.

Of course, not everyone agreed with my conclusion. My analysis of the system problem was met with mixed reviews. Some teachers and administrators were keenly aware that there was something wrong. Many confessed that they did their best work in spite of the system; the factory model forced them to resort to guerilla warfare. But there were many more who took issue with the selecting premise.

I saw it each time I stood before an audience and began to make my case. There was a marked shift in body language. Facial expressions changed. Teachers, administrators, and board members who minutes before were cheering at the blueberry story and laughing at the smelly eighth graders suddenly seized up. They folded their arms across their chests. The laughter stopped. And during the ensuing Q&A, a chorus of voices rose up, singing variations on the following theme:

> Hold on there, Bub! I'm not selecting and sorting in my classroom! I care about all these kids, sometimes more than their parents. I'm showing up here every day and working myself to the point of exhaustion to prepare them for the challenges they face. You've got a lot of gall to come in here and tell me I'm just sorting these kids.

I heard this coast to coast.

I knew that most of them were dedicated professionals. I knew that their days were long, their compensation was inadequate, and they deserved to be praised every day. But I also knew that all of them were selecting and sorting their students whether they wanted to or not. I knew this not because I was so smart or because I had access to privileged information. I knew it because there was a smoking gun—a flaw sitting right in the middle of the education process exposed for all to see. An insidious fact of daily life in America's schools that was built into the system centuries before any of us were born. An aspect of standard operating procedure that absolutely guarantees that everyone working in our schools, despite their best efforts, selects and sorts their students every day. The problem is huge and unbelievably problematic, but it can be described in four words: we hold time constant.

Chapter 7

The Smoking Gun

You walk in; you get injected, inspected,
detected, infected, neglected and selected.

Arlo Guthrie

All children go to school the same number of hours and the same number of days. This fact alone confirms that we are sorting children as opposed to educating them to their highest levels of achievement. And every parent and every teacher knows why: because some children take longer to learn than others, for reasons that can have little to do with intelligence. In fact, there is no research that equates the speed at which someone learns with his or her ability or capacity to learn. Some children just need more time.

Some children are more thoughtful and deliberative. Some have undetected physical problems that interfere with concentration. Some children are not as mentally or emotionally ready to learn simply because they are younger than their classmates—sometimes by as much as a year at a point in their development when even six months is an eternity. Some children start with less prior knowledge than their peers. Some are highly stressed, living in dreadful conditions marked by neglect or abuse. Some have been deliberately taught by their parents to resist their teachers because they are the enemy. Some are sleep deprived. Some learn best in a real world context. For myriad reasons, human beings learn at different rates of speed. And as long as we choose to hold time constant for teaching, learning, and testing, we are sorting children not on the basis of their intelligence, but on the basis of that speed.

It's a race.

Each year millions of students, grouped according to age, line up and step into the starting blocks. The opening bell rings. And they're off! The clock begins to tick, tick, tick, and everyone feels the pressure.

Teachers feel it. They have dozens of units to teach, and they know that their evaluations are influenced by their ability to "cover the content." Pacing guides drive their action forward whether or not all of their students have mastered the material. The relentless ticking forces them to teach to the middle.

Principals feel it. Each year they watch their workloads expand as legislators and bureaucrats raise academic standards, expand the number of mandates, and demand greater accountability for results while never adding a minute to the school calendar.

Students feel it. Each spring they get swept up in the mad dash for the finish line, and they wonder aloud, "Why do they keep printing the last five chapters in our textbooks? We never get to them!"

The big school clock has been ticking for decades, but the testing hysteria that has swept the nation in the last eight years has intensified the pressure. Preparation for these high stake tests steals time and squeezes the schedule, making it nearly impossible for all students to learn what they really need to know to prosper as adults.

Day in and day out for nine months, the battle of the clock continues. The students who make it to graduation day wind up distributed across a chart like this:

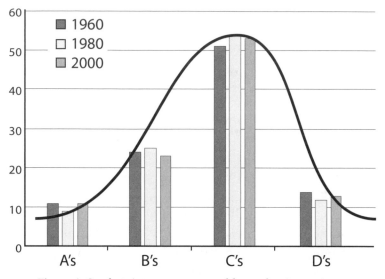

Figure 4. Grade point averages earned by graduating seniors at a typical American high school sampled over 40 years.

This is the end product of the selecting process: a classic bell curve—some excellence, some failure, and shades of average in between. As long as we hold time constant, the selecting system will produce this distribution of student achievement. *Every time.* This does not mean that teachers cannot, through extraordinary effort and personal sacrifice, overcome the constraints and make a difference for an individual child. The story of Miss Skelton and my dad is testimony to that. But the selecting forces of the system are inexorable. No matter how hard they work, or how much they care, when it comes to most kids, our teachers and administrators are at the mercy of the iron rule:

TIME CONSTANT.
LEARNING VARIABLE.

Of course, prior to the 1990s there was nothing wrong with this outcome, at least from the perspective of the economy. Most people found jobs—pretty darn good jobs—regardless of their class rank.

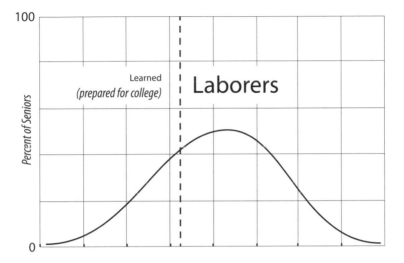

Figure 5. Traditional Bell Curve.

As we have seen, however, the challenges presented by the knowledge-based economy require a very different outcome. Being educated "well enough" is measured against rigorous benchmarks. Now, learning must be the constant. Our schools must produce a new curve. (See Figure 6.)

The present system cannot do this.

Holding time constant may be the most conspicuous aspect of the selecting process, but it isn't the only one. There are serious impediments to student success related to when, where, how, and what we teach. Until we accept the fact that the core system is the primary problem, we will never create schools that teach all children to high levels. Until we tackle head-on the selecting premise that sits at the heart of the system, we will never get the graduates we need.

ℰℭ

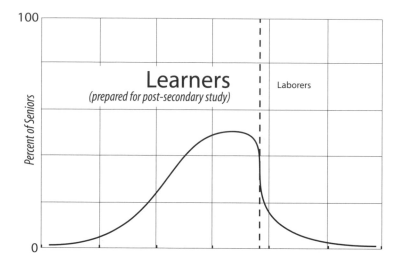

Figure 6. The new curve.

I was sure that my analysis of time and curves and our changing society was conclusive on the need for change. Once again, however, not everyone agreed. I was met with a barrage of tortured defenses of the status quo. But the one that I heard the most was summed up in two words: So what?

> So there's a curve. What's the problem? We give all kids the same material, we give them the same amount of time to learn, we teach them in the same conditions, and then we test them the same way. At the end of the day, we find out who's smart and who's not. And it's in our interest to do it fast. The earlier we can sort them the easier it is to allocate resources accordingly. The system works, Jamie. It's a meritocracy, and it is totally fair. Get a grip!

I heard variations on this theme in corporate boardrooms, faculty lounges, Little League bleachers, five star restaurants, and corner diners across the country. I even heard it from some of the same people who had initially denied that they were sorting kids, which made me feel as though I was trying to hit a moving target.

Initially, I was taken aback. Not because it seemed callous— the truth is not always pleasant—but because the conclusion was at odds with a mountain of established facts about teaching and learning, and it ignored common experience. Given our needs, it also seemed fatalistic.

After asking a lot of questions, I realized that the acceptance of the status quo was based on three core beliefs:

> Belief #1 – Intelligence is genetic and immutable. People are born with a certain amount of general intelligence (*g*), and this level is fixed for life.

> Belief #2 – Intelligence is distributed across a bell curve. In any population of significant size, e.g., a high school class, there is some genius, some rubbish, and a whole lot of average in between.

> Belief #3 – The bell curve of human intelligence and the bell curve of student achievement are, for all practical purposes, the same curve. The most intelligent students get As, the average kids get Cs, and the least intelligent get Fs. The curves match almost perfectly because our schools are doing an excellent job of sorting the groups.

These three beliefs regarding the nature of human intelligence are key to understanding our predicament. If they are grounded in fact, then the defenders of the status quo are right: the system is sound. Sure, we can tweak the schedule and maybe raise the achievement of some marginal kids, and, of course, all the people working in the schools can work harder, but there is no need for major reform; our schools are effectively and efficiently identifying the genius and the rubbish. If, on the other hand, any of these core beliefs are groundless, then the selecting premise is indefensible, and we face a systems problem of enormous proportions. All three seemed plausible, but I had to establish the truth before I could proceed.

So far, I had been extremely lucky in my pursuit of answers. From my earliest days with the Roundtable, it seemed as though the hand of Fate had been dealing me cards off the bottom of the deck. Generous, knowledgeable people and opportunities to learn appeared out of nowhere throughout my informal education. This pattern continued when I was invited to attend the annual conference of the American Educational Research Association in New York City. By this point, I had learned to follow the signs, and I eagerly accepted. By the end of the first day, however, I had begun to wonder what the heck I was doing there: the sessions were interesting, but none seemed relevant to my pursuit. Then I wandered into a session where Harvard professor Howard Gardner was speaking and I knew I'd struck a vein.

This was my introduction to the theories of the "cognitive revolution." I took a seat in the front row.

In the months that followed, I found the research and analysis (that I could decipher) to be both intellectually satisfying and consistent with my experience. It was not long before I realized that of the three core beliefs listed above, #1 and #3 were flat-out wrong, and #2 was correct, but only if I thought of the bell curve in three dimensions, not two.

Chapter 8

Challenging the Core Beliefs

"The status quo sucks."

George Carlin

Humans have been thinking about the nature of intelligence for a long time. The oldest surviving texts addressing the subject were written in India seven millennia ago, and there was a rich oral tradition long before that. In the last forty years, however, a revolution has occurred, and we have discovered more about the mechanics of the brain and the nature of human intelligence than we learned in all of recorded history. People working in biology, neuroscience, linguistics, education, computer science, anthropology, sociology, philosophy, and psychology have come together to probe the innate ability that powers human learning. To draw their conclusions, they use scientific method, computer simulation, modeling, and the latest techniques of manipulating and observing the microscopic activities of the brain. Their findings can sometimes seem incredible, and they produce a sense of wonder, but they have profound, practical implications.

Their most stunning discovery, at least in the context of my exploration, is that intelligence grows; it is not fixed or immutable. Contrary to the conventional wisdom expressed in Belief #1, the brain is not akin to a machine that is permanently hardwired in the first few years of life. It is changing and organic. With the right environmental stimuli, the brain's neural connections can grow both in number and complexity, and the lines of communication that carry information between neurons can become more efficient. In the right circumstances, the brain can perfect its own circuits so it is better able to learn.

This phenomenon is known as "neural plasticity," and its discovery has been heralded as a great leap in human history, greater even than stepping on the moon. But whether or not such claims are true, what is absolutely clear is that the assertion that "you've either got big g or you don't" is not true. Intelligence can grow, and, more to the point, schools can actively accelerate the growth process by providing learning environments and programs that stimulate the development of neural connections.[3]

The hard evidence of the changing brain was (and remains) a huge challenge to the "so what" defenders of the status quo, but it wasn't only Belief #1 that was under attack. Within the same cognitive revolution, there was a different group of scientists who were challenging Belief #2: they were questioning the nature, even the existence, of the bell curve.

The principal line of attack came from the theory of multiple intelligences (MI). This concept emerged from the interplay of developmental psychology and behavioral science. In broad terms, MI theory holds that there is not just one monolithic intelligence that can be measured by standardized verbal instruments, ranked in order of magnitude, and plotted across a single curve. Rather, there are eight separate and distinct types of intelligence distributed across eight separate curves. The eight identified are:

---

[3] I found one of the more innovative programs in the schools across the country that have introduced two short periods of research-based Transcendental Meditation into the daily schedule. During these "quiet times," students meditating at their desks with their eyes closed for just fifteen minutes settle down and display increased brainwave coherence in the prefrontal cortex. Longitudinal studies have linked this coherence to a marked increase in neural connections and a permanent increase in student IQ.

Linguistic Intelligence
Logical/Mathematical Intelligence
Musical Intelligence
Spatial Intelligence
Bodily/Kinesthetic Intelligence
Interpersonal Intelligence
Intrapersonal Intelligence
Naturalistic Intelligence

According to MI theory, every human being possesses a unique combination of some or all of these distinct cognitive abilities. In his 1983 book *Frames of Mind*, Professor Howard Gardner called these combinations "profiles of intelligence." He maintains that each profile is akin to a natural resource waiting to be mined. Each profile contains creativity and energy that can propel an individual to solve problems and/or create products that are valued by society. Each profile, properly developed, can be a wellspring of insight and innovation.

There was an element of common sense in the theory, but I initially approached this research with enormous skepticism. Society has accepted the theory of the bell curve of general intelligence for a long time, and while it is true that major paradigms can suddenly shift, it doesn't happen often. I knew many smart people who seemed to succeed in almost everything, and I knew others, like my next door neighbor, who convinced me that there was a curve every time they opened their mouths. I was loath to abandon the concept.

What finally turned me around was a comment by a friend—a poet of all people—who said, "You're thinking about it the wrong way. You don't have to abandon the sacred bell. Just think of it in broader terms. Think of it as a real bell."

It was then that I began to see that the MI theories were not a repudiation of the traditional understanding, but an important elaboration. Human intelligence *is* distributed across a curve, but the curve is not a two-dimensional line. It is a three-dimensional bell comprised of as many two-dimensional curves as there are individual profiles of intelligence. The true bell curve of human intelligence looks like this:

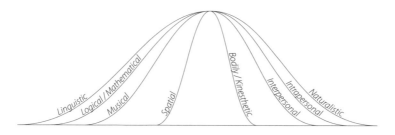

Figure 7. Three-Dimensional Bell.

Slice the bell along any axis, and each cross section will reveal a different "traditional" two-dimensional bell curve with human beings distributed from front to back. Where an individual sits on the curve may and, most likely, will change depending upon the line that is exposed. For example, if we cut along the Linguistic axis, a person may be positioned near the front of the bell.

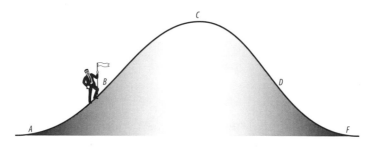

Figure 8. Cross section on Linguistic axis.

The same person, however, may sit in an entirely different, even opposite, position when the Mathematical axis is exposed.

Figure 9. Cross section on Mathematics axis.
Any similarity between this example and the author's profile is purely coincidental.

The three-dimensional bell accounts for all human beings and the full range of human intelligence. It is a very satisfying concept. The 3-D bell also shows that the traditional way of thinking about the curve as expressed in Belief #2, while not wrong, is much too narrow. And this insight immediately focused my attention on Belief #3.

Recall that adherents of Belief #3 maintain that the bell curve of human intelligence and the bell curve of student achievement represented in Figure 4 are essentially the same curve: the people at the front of the GPA curve are the most intelligent; the people at the back are the least. If, however, there are multiple curves of intelligence, then a momentous question arises: exactly which slice of the bell does the GPA chart represent? Which geniuses have we been identifying and rewarding? Who have we been labeling and discarding as rubbish? Just what in heaven's name have we been selecting for all these years?

This question has revolutionary implications. The answer has the potential to set the entire country on a course that will completely transform our schools. And it turns out that anyone who has been to school—any school—knows what the answer is.

It is the curve that reveals how young people adapt to sitting in rows for long hours under close supervision. It is the curve that shows us how students cope with a daily schedule shattered by constant interruption; a schedule that forces them to move at the sound of a bell from workstation to workstation, boss to boss, carrying their books and supplies. It is the curve that tells us how our kids—some who must be medicated to stay focused—respond to a curriculum that breaks the whole of human knowledge into pieces presented in an arbitrary sequence by teachers who have little chance to collaborate; a curriculum that asks our kids to create meaning out of a steady stream of unrelated, seemingly irrelevant facts that may or may not help them make sense of their world. It is the curve that shows how kids handle conventional teaching methods favoring visual and auditory learners with long attention spans. It is the curve that exposes the fate of children with different learning styles, the ones who become frustrated and angry and slowly drift to the back of the class where the system literally adds insult to injury by labeling them as "losers." Finally, it is the curve that reveals how students respond to assessment instruments that favor those who can memorize heaps of discrete facts, store them in short-term memory, and recall them on demand during an assortment of timed tests.

Stated in its simplest form, it's the curve that shows us just one thing: *how well our kids do in school.* Which means that the only way that Belief #3 is valid, the only possible way that the curve of student achievement is the same as the curve of human intelligence, is if we define intelligence in very narrow terms. And in a world where our individual and collective fates are linked to our ability to capture all the brainpower we can get, narrowly defining intelligence is something we can no longer afford to do.

଼ଓଓ

The cognitive revolution was still in its infancy when I wandered in, and there were plenty of critics who dismissed the theories as no more than speculative judgments. There was, however, enough empirical evidence from enough reputable sources to convince me that a new understanding of the nature of intelligence was at hand that eviscerated any defense of the status quo. Each new insight seemed to proclaim with more urgency that the system needed to change.

On a personal note, the new theories helped explain my experiences as a father of three bright children who had very different experiences in school: one Logical-Mathematical whiz who breezed through the system on her way to the Ivy League; one Linguistic/Interpersonal dreamer, with blue sky in his eyes and ants-in-his-pants, who fought the system tooth and nail from the first day he was told to sit down and be quiet; and one Bodily/Kinesthetic dancer who had to move to think, and who never quite fit in anywhere until after she graduated. The expanded version of the bell also helped explain the adult fortunes of my three best friends and classmates at George Washington High in Philadelphia. All three were average students, at best, but they went on to become successful in the arts, medicine, and business. Especially Richie. He hated school. He read constantly, but never the assignments. He got nothing but Cs and Ds, and now, as the owner of a software company, he employs rooms filled with people who got As, and he has become filthy rich in the process. Creep.

What was not explained by my investigation was why we as a nation of smart, practical people have put up with the selecting system for so long. Yes it served the economy, but I wasn't convinced that this fact alone was reason enough for so much denial. Why, for example, have we accepted the bizarre, distinctly American notion that it's totally okay for millions of us to have forgotten most of what we learned in school? Why have we compartmentalized the experiences of so many of our friends and neighbors who didn't begin to be successful until after they got out of school? Why have we accepted a one-size-fits-all system that overlooks the obvious differences in student backgrounds, levels of readiness, and learning styles? Why have we gone to such great lengths to support a system patently designed to leave children behind?

I would find the answers to these questions in the weeks and months to come. They would show me why Americans were not ready to accept the wholesale restructuring of their schools. They would stimulate my earliest thinking about the need for The Great Conversation, and they would prompt the writing of this book.

At this point in my journey, however, all I knew for sure was that I was not the man I was. I was no longer a victim of my own blinkered thinking, false assumptions, and impatience. I took some comfort in knowing that there had never been anything wrong with my original objective. My oft-repeated calls to change our schools had been appropriate and timely. It was my arguments that had been wrong—ill-informed and simplistic. And, of course, my belligerent tone had been flat-out destructive. I decided to step back, stop traveling, and organize everything I had learned. My goal was to create a new presentation that would help my professional and lay audiences understand why our schools must change, and why it was important that everyone support the process. [4]

I structured the case in five parts built on a central rationale: when it comes to educating America's children, we are experiencing a unique and auspicious convergence of what's right and what's necessary. We must end the selecting process and redesign the system to unfold the full creative potential of every child in all its forms.

• Part One offered a short history lesson designed to show how the nation's early one-room schools grew to become the complex, multifaceted, overburdened institutions that exist today.

---

[4] I gave the finished product the catchy title, *Why Our Schools Need to Change*. The following year I produced a thirty-minute video of the same name.

• Part Two described the changing needs of the American economy, the demise of the two-tiered world of work, and our need to position all children for some sort of post-secondary education. Instead of citing the pressures of the economy as reasons to "improve" the system, I argued that those same pressures were now reasons to end it.

• Part Three explained the need for change for reasons that had nothing to do with the workplace. I juxtaposed the relative simplicity of daily life in the industrial era with the growing complexity of life in the knowledge age to demonsrtate that today's students needed to develop high levels functional literacy just to survive.

• Part Four provided a very basic introduction to the cognitive revolution including the discovery of neural plasticity and the existence of multiple profiles of intelligence. Unlike Part Two, which used the economic argument to prove that the selecting system was ineffective, Part Four used our new understanding of the nature of intelligence to prove that the system was unjust.

• Part Five was a summation and a call to arms. I restated that our schools were designed for a vanishing society and based on mistaken beliefs about potential. I argued that it was madness to demand that teachers and administrators work harder within a flawed system and expect a different result. And I insisted that the time had come for all of us to come together to replace the rigid, factory-like, selecting and sorting system with schools that prepared all children to become confident, successful, responsible American adults.

At no point did I state what the restructured system should look like. This disappointed some people who wanted "the answer," but it was my experience that promoting specific reforms was how outsiders—even informed outsiders—got themselves in trouble. I was sure that we needed to redesign—not reinforce or reform—the entrenched system with the ultimate goal of unfolding the full potential of every child. And it seemed plausible that we should build a multidimensional approach to learning that was flexible from the perspectives of time, teaching style, and assessment. But I didn't kid myself. I knew that I had neither the credentials nor the experience to offer detailed prescriptions.

I saw my role in narrow terms. I believed that I could combine my business background with everything I had learned about how our schools worked to help raise awareness of the need for change and inspire people to become involved. Above all, I felt the pressure to act. The transformation from agrarian-age schools to industrial-age schools had taken over a hundred years. There was no way that we had that kind of time to redesign our schools for the knowledge age. The pace of global change was accelerating. Our children needed action now, and I was eager to contribute.

After months of private reflection, I was ready to put my message to the test. The trick would be to get someone to listen.

PART III

The Public Is Not Ready

Chapter 9

Struggling to Be Heard

A good listener is not only popular everywhere,
but after a while he knows something.

Wilson Mizne

Anyone attempting to change public education faces an uphill battle just to get his or her message heard. The institution is big and culturally entrenched. Most educators are overburdened. They are highly insular and speak their own language despite the fact that their schools sit in the geographic and cultural centers of their communities. The controlling bureaucracy is highly proscriptive. Hundreds of interacting and conflicting rules and regulations generate a white noise that jams incoming signals.

And these are just the major obstacles in plain view. Many of the impediments I encountered are less obvious to the untrained eye, but no less effective in frustrating meaningful communication, starting with the venues.

The physical settings in which I made my presentations hardly improved my chances for success. For those in the know, two words say it all: in-service days. Better than two thirds of the calls I received from superintendents invited me to speak during these interesting events. My only prior experience with professional development programs was as an attorney. Continuing Legal Education courses were usually staged in dignified surroundings, and

I attended at my convenience. Each one offered a menu of practical topics, and I had the option to choose the sessions I deemed most relevant to my work. The contrast with a typical district in-service program was striking.

Most sessions were held on site, often in open areas euphemistically called "the commons." These spaces had all the amenities of a school's cafeteria: hard chairs, harsh lighting, and dreadful acoustics. Too many times to count, I struggled to be heard over banks of vending machines as their wheezing compressors cycled on and off. The rooms were either freezing or a hundred degrees. Refreshments, if any, included tepid coffee and high-fat donuts or sweet rolls brought in from the local market. Attendance was mandatory for all certified employees, and yet the presentations often failed to address the immediate needs of anyone in the audience. And even when they did, there was rarely any opportunity for in-depth discussion or group interaction.

As always, time was tight. So it was common for these sessions to be grafted onto the end of a busy day when everyone was already tired. Some programs were scheduled during normal school hours, which necessitated either a late start or an early release of students. On these occasions, parents had to scramble for childcare, and all the teachers knew they were paying a price with the community.

Very little of this was the result of mismanagement or neglect on the part of administrators. The sad truth was that most professional development budgets were miniscule, and they remain so today. Americans take it for granted that their doctors and lawyers regularly update their knowledge and skills, but teachers are expected to either know everything they need to know when they graduate from college or keep abreast of latest developments on the fly. The prevailing attitude was succinctly encapsulated in a comment I heard at a local coffee shop prior to one of my talks: "If those teachers aren't in the classroom with the kids, then they're not earning their pay." With this as the public's mindset, it's no surprise that opportunities for teachers to engage in deep listening and learning are rare.

Over time, I grew to appreciate, even enjoy, these sessions, and they most definitely forced me to hone my presentation skills, but the dominant professional development milieu made a tough job even tougher.

Of course, the fact that I am an outsider didn't help. The system reacts to change agents like me the way the human body reacts to a virus: the immune system goes into high gear mode to kill the intruder. I may have fancied myself an informed friend and advocate with a pro-education message, but that didn't mean I was embraced with open arms. Friendly or not, I was still an outsider, and any call to change from someone with little or no classroom experience was greeted with suspicion, at best.

A middle school principal in Virginia said it best:

> We are already awash in "expert" solutions that are created by professors, codified by politicians, and enforced by bureaucrats. I call this triumvirate the "Axis of Chaos." They rarely consult any of us who work with kids during the development of their programs, which makes us feel more like objects of reform than partners in the process. Most of the time, their programs offer simplistic solutions for complex problems, and complex solutions for simple problems. And they always, always produce mountains of paperwork. We are left to conclude that few members of the Axis have ever actually had to make their programs work, and we're the ones who have to clean up the mess when they don't. All this makes us more than a bit leery of someone like you.

To be fair, the general response to my revised presentation was a huge improvement over my blueberry reception. I never encountered overt hostility. Most people were listening, and they refrained from grading papers in front of me. (Every now and then I got a standing ovation, but that only happened if they had been sitting on metal chairs for two hours.) But even when it was going well, the vibe in the room always warped when I broached the subject of change. Their faces remained impassive, but I could almost hear everyone in the audience groaning, "Oh, please. Not again."

It was hard to blame them. Generations of critics have decried little Johnny's inability to read, write, and do basic math, and each new round of condemnation unleashes a new wave of reform. Over the course of their careers, the veterans in my audiences had been swept up in dozens of "must do" programs. A partial list includes: Child-Centered Classrooms, Content-Centered Curriculum, New Math, New Physics, New Chemistry, Open-Classrooms, Whole Language, Direct Instruction, Engaged Learning, Purpose-Centered Education, Reading First, Modern Red Schoolhouse, Paideia, Expeditionary Learning, ATLAS Communities, Urban Learning Centers, Co-NECT, Foxfire Fund, Core Knowledge, Roots and Wings, Different Ways of Knowing, Success for All, Onward to Excellence, Minimum Competency Testing, Error-Oriented Teaching, Teaching to Think, Outcomes Based Education, Total Quality Education, Computer Assisted Instruction, and, of course, the standards-based/high-stakes testing initiatives required by No Child Left Behind.

As a former ice cream man I refer to this process as, *"Flavor O' the Month Reform."* The comparison is apt: many of the programs disappear as fast as a scoop of mint chip on a hot summer day. No reform, however, is nearly as satisfying.

There were times when I suspected that there were teachers and administrators in my audience who agreed with my assessment of the selecting problem. Many longed for something different. But it was hard to be receptive to someone who had never spent a minute in their shoes—someone just passing through. For the truth was that I would be gone in an hour, and they would return to face rooms filled with demanding kids, and fight a mind-numbing bureaucracy that was slowing driving them insane.

There was one more barrier to receptivity that, while rarely mentioned, was always in the room. It had to do with money.

Every educator knows that Americans invest in the things they value. They hear plenty of talk in the public arena about how important it is that we teach all children to high levels, and how critical teachers are to the education process. A reasonable person could conclude that their budgets and salaries would reflect the public's professed regard for teaching and learning. But as they sit and listen to me review the competitive pressures of the global market, most teachers know that they are paid less per capita than their peers in developed and some not-so-developed countries. They also know that they earn less than other professionals in America who have less education and, arguably, less demanding or important jobs. Politicians, journalists, and business people like me can promote the need to restructure our schools, but with each paycheck, with every failed bond referendum, teachers, administrators, and board members get the message loud and clear: when it comes to demanding world-class schools, talk is cheap.

Given the impediments presented by the bureaucracy, the venue, the history, and societal indifference, it was no surprise that public school employees were hesitant to embrace any call to reform, no matter how logically presented or passionately expressed. I've heard their critics in business, politics, and the media condemn this response as an act of "rank obstinacy": a self-serving intransigence enabled by unions, tenure, and the lack of competition. There was a time when I agreed. I have learned, however, that it is not true. My experiences with teachers, administrators, support staff, and board members have convinced me that a lifetime of bad experiences has taught them to listen to talk of reform with more fear than hope. Their collective response is not intransigence; it is a learned survival skill that is better characterized as "tempered skepticism."

I am quick to acknowledge that there are some teachers and administrators whose response is less rational. I call them the T.T.S.P. people. Years of exposure to ill-conceived, ineffective, stop-and-start reforms have left them closed minded and crabby. And easy to spot. Anytime someone utters the expression, "We have to change," their jaws clench, their eyes squint, and their spines stretch like a taut bow. One overriding thought fills their minds:

> I'm not changing. I'm good at what I do. I was doing it long before you got here and I'll be doing it long after you are gone. I'm going to ignore you and your ideas. I'm going back to my room, close my door, and do my job. Just make sure I have the supplies I need, give me a shot at the copy machine that's locked up in the principal's office, and leave me alone. I'm not changing nothing! You know why? Because This Too Shall Pass![5]

In truth, every educator carries a trace of the T.T.S.P. response in his or her blood. It is an occupational hazard. (Of course, the heaviest concentrations are found among high school teachers because, let's face it, most of them think that they're independent contractors.) But, against all odds, and despite all the nasty rhetoric and waves of dead-end reform they have endured, the seriously deranged are a small minority. The vast majority of teachers, administrators, board members, and support staff are acutely aware that not all children are well served, and most are willing to undertake the substantial changes required to increase student success.

---

[5] Those of you who fit this profile need not stand up and testify. Everyone knows who you are.

ॐ ☙

As the 1990s came to a close, I was finally sure that I was being heard. Administrators were eager to expose their staffs and communities to the message. I was traveling tens of thousands of miles per year. I spoke in the media centers (libraries) in tiny rural elementary schools. I stood on magnificent stages in rich suburban high schools. I did my best to connect with severely stressed teachers and administrators in the inner city for whom the prospect of meaningful change seemed pretty remote.

Everywhere I went, positive feedback replaced anger and skepticism. Change agents and "early adopters" hung around at the end of my talks to thank me for the reinforcement. Administrators and board members talked about what they could do next. A teacher in western Kansas stopped me cold when he said that he had decided to quit the profession, but my message had changed his mind. I was humbled by the response and grateful for the encouragement, but I was not in it for the strokes. What kept me going were the signs I saw of real change. Progress was far from universal, but I began to see districts where motivated leaders were positioning themselves and their staffs to rethink and restructure their schools. They were attacking the system with one overriding goal: to increase student success. And they were not tinkering at the edges.

Chapter 10

On the Brink of Progress

We can't solve problems by using the same kind
of thinking we used when we created them.

Albert Einstein

L et's be clear: the changes I saw had little to do with me. The
pressure to improve was coming at schools from all direc-
tions. The firestorm of condemnation that followed the release of
A Nation at Risk in 1983 set the stage for President George H.W.
Bush's America 2000 agenda, which then morphed into President
Clinton's Goals 2000 agenda. Headlines warned of the threats
posed by the educational achievements of our international competitors. Millions of American workers watched helplessly as the
outsourcing of jobs decimated entire industries. The implosion
of the dot.com bubble in early 2000 scared the bejeepers out of
everyone, and, as so often happens in times of national stress,
schools became the scapegoat.

Districts responded to the pressures by focusing on four areas
of concern.

First, they were tackling the **curriculum**.

Leaders in progressive districts had accepted a fundamental
truth: their schools could not be all things to all people and hope
to survive. Even a cursory review of the curriculum revealed that
it had become a mile wide and an inch deep—fragmented, calci-

fied, with no overarching purpose. To remedy the problem they put together a coalition of local stakeholders and charged them with answering what I think is the single most important question: what do our graduates need to know and be able to do to when they graduate? By working locally, they tacitly acknowledged one of my core beliefs: the farther the decision maker is from the child, the dumber the decision gets.

Coalition members were guided by three organizing principles. Number one, they were going to have to engage in some constructive abandonment; it was not possible or necessary to teach their students everything that their parents *and grandparents* were taught, plus everything that had happened since. Number two, the answer was not as simple as, "Just give 'em the basics." Everyone accepted the fact that teaching the 3Rs was essential, but they also knew that the curriculum had to promote the 3Ts: thinking, technology, and teamwork skills. Only by mastering these new basics would their students develop the functional literacy they needed to succeed as adults. And number three, reinventing the wheel was not required. They could use existing content standards and recommendations from reputable sources as *guidelines*, choosing the curricular pieces that made the most sense for their children and their circumstances.

Second, smart districts were addressing the perennial problem of **student motivation.**

District leaders realized that creating an appropriate curriculum was less than half the battle. They had to motivate their students to actually learn what the curriculum contained. Young people who were plugged into a culture that fostered attention spans measured in minutes, if not seconds, had to be motivated to engage in a process with feedback loops measured in weeks, months, and years. The best leaders knew that it was unreasonable to expect all teachers to be spellbinding orators. They also knew that constantly threatening and cajoling students was never going to work. The key to increasing motivation lay in changing the nature of the work that students were asked to do. To paraphrase the great educational leader Phil Schlecty, teachers and administrators had to develop lessons and assignments that linked the things students cared about to the things they needed to learn, if they were ever to inspire student fascination, or, at the very, least sustained interest.

To accomplish this goal, plans were set in motion to expand and subsidize high-quality professional development, i.e., to replace anemic, periodic in-service programs with robust, ongoing development streams through which practical knowledge could flow from proven sources with records of success. The objective was not to magically turn all teachers into some combination of movie star and pop diva delivering lessons in a video game format. Rather, the aim was to provide each member of the staff—regardless of personality type—with the relevant knowledge, lessons, and practical skills he or she needed to harness each student's innate impulse to learn.

Third, these districts were rethinking *assessment*. And it was in this arena that I found the most energy and agreement.

Everyone accepted the need to accurately measure and clearly report student achievement. Everyone I spoke with was willing to be held accountable for his or her results. And almost everyone expressed frustration with the growing hysteria of standardized testing. They understood the political appeal of norm-referenced tests. But teachers, administrators, and board members alike declared, often in heated language, that these tests were perverting teaching and learning, and, worse, they were directly at odds with their attempts to increase student motivation. The consensus was that low-bid, machine-scored "bubble tests" penalized rather than capitalized on student variability, and, further, that the high-stakes nature of these "gatekeeper" tests reinforced the worst features of the selecting system. Everyone knew that they couldn't ignore the tests, but they were determined to create flexible approaches to assessment that recognized that children "test" differently. No was one suggesting a compromise on the issue of rigor—all students would be required to learn challenging material—but proponents of the change argued that classroom teachers could augment standardized tests with a balanced program of portfolio assessment, and in doing so, produce reliable results that could be clearly reported to the public.

Of course, this last point raised the highly sensitive issue of changing report cards. The most aggressive districts were considering alternative report cards that would explain a student's strengths and weaknesses in clear, unambiguous terms, and, most importantly, chart a child's progress from year to year. Parents would be better able to gauge their child's development, and taxpayers would be able to see for themselves if they were getting the bang for the buck they deserved. It was an idea fraught with risk, but long overdue.

Finally, in addition to curriculum, motivation, and assessment, these brave agents of change were rethinking the scariest issue of all: the *school calendar*.

They approached the topic by asking what schedule would best serve the goal of increasing student success. To the greatest extent possible, they sought to apply the latest knowledge of the physical and mental development of school-age children. They started with the mounting evidence that a child's earliest experiences—birth to age four—profoundly shaped the architecture of the brain. In response, committees were formed to consider strengthening and expanding early childhood programs that cultivated both cognitive and behavioral skills. Longitudinal studies were considered that linked participation in such programs to lower special education rates, less need for remediation and retention, and higher graduation rates. These studies found that benefits could exceed costs by as much as seventeen to one.

In the upper grades, alternative schedules were being considered based on neuro-biological data that suggested that the parameters of the traditional school day—when it started and ended—were severely out of sync with adolescent metabolisms. (Hardly news to any parent who's ever watched a teenager stagger out of bed for school.)

Really aggressive districts were rethinking the entire school calendar. They were specifically questioning the wisdom of adhering to a schedule created to serve an agro-industrial society that had ceased to exist—a schedule that had not appreciably changed since World War II. Planners recognized that there was no perfect schedule: some models added days; some extended the length of the traditional day; some redistributed the standard 180 days throughout the year. The common feature of each alternative was greater flexibility and increased opportunities for remediation and enrichment. (As a businessman, I was pleased to see a growing acceptance of the principles of continuous improvement.) The objective was to create a schedule that would ensure that the greatest number of students reached the articulated goals.

No one district was moving forward on all four fronts, but all were contemplating fundamental changes to the existing system. They were intent on overcoming institutional inertia to create focused, flexible, high-expectation learning environments that capitalized on human variability and developed the creative intelligence of all students.

I was very pleased to see that a handful of districts recognized that their schools could not do it alone—there were too many out-of-school factors to surmount. Their leaders were beginning to form partnerships with health professionals, social service agencies, civic and business leaders, and the clergy with the express goal of creating programs that would support the mental, physical, and emotional well-being of every child.

With diligence and determination, these districts worked to

create the infrastructure and practices that would lead to student success. Members of the staff and the school board formed study groups, went to conferences, and worked with consultants. Representatives of each part of the system met together on their own time before and after school seated around tables piled high with notebooks, case studies, carbohydrates, and caffeine. They read and thought and talked and argued. They took great pains to stay practical, and to align their plans with the needs of their kids. They were thoughtful and thorough.

And after twelve to eighteen months of intense effort calculated to change their schools for the better forever, do you know what happened in these districts?

Nothing.

Oh, not quite nothing. Something happened. A war broke out. The leaders found themselves besieged by resistant staffs and angry forces in the community who were dead-set against change. District plans were misunderstood by some and deliberately misrepresented by others. Bitter talk of hidden agendas and personal vendettas combined to antagonize the staff and polarize the community. The war of words escalated until finally reaching a crescendo during the next school board election, when three or four angry candidates launched "anti-everything" platforms heavily laced with fear and innuendo. For weeks, adversarial factions lobbed charge and countercharge. And on election night, when the votes were counted, the resisters won, fracturing the board, and bringing all plans for change to a shrieking halt.

It was a mess. The change agents who had labored to move their schools forward were drained and disillusioned with little to show for their effort. The negative trolls and the T.T.S.P. crowd in the teachers' lounges sneered, "See, we told you we shouldn't have done this." Community members with and without kids in school were angry and confused. Months of hard work had come and gone, and the only thing that permanently changed in these districts was … the superintendent.

I watched this scene unfold again and again in districts from coast to coast, and I simply did not get it. Why was this happening? Dedicated people who had slogged away to improve the system were being clubbed from behind by reactionary forces in the community. Why would the public resist changes that would result in greater student success? It made no sense.

I was mystified at first, and angry. But as the failures mounted, a pattern began to emerge. And right in the middle, driving the action and causing so much trouble, was an archaic notion of "real school."

Chapter 11

The Obstructive Power of "Real School"

We have met the enemy, and he is us.

Walt Kelly

Anyone who has ever worked in a large organization knows that many terrific initiatives die in the planning. Peter Senge, in his 1990 book *The Fifth Discipline*, argues that this failure to put new ideas into practice comes not from a lack of will or effort, but, in part, from the existence of "mental models." The people who will be affected by the changes have deeply held internal images of how the system works, and they resist innovations that conflict with those ideas. I spoke with Dr. Senge once, and I started to tell him what I did for a living. Before I could finish my sentence he said, "I can think of few mental models in this country that are more deeply entrenched and rigid than the public's model of school." In the years since that conversation, I have come to realize that his assessment was probably an understatement.

Like most mental models, the ones associated with K-12 education are generally subconscious and unexamined, and yet they govern our thinking and behavior. The dominant model is detailed, emotionally charged, and, unfortunately, a precise replica of a system that is highly flawed.

In fairness, it is all we know. Almost all of us passed through the selecting process no matter where we went to school. We were very young and impressionable when we started. We spent years navigating the halls, responding to the bells, moving through the crazy sequences, and trying to make sense of the nonstop torrent of abstractions. We left as teenagers, and few of us have ever gone back to the classroom for more than an awkward visit. The sights, sounds, and smells lie deep within our consciousness. Our memories—clear and fuzzy, good and bad—have merged over the decades to form pictures and stories of "the way school ought to be." Ask most people what they think their schools should look like and the answer is simple: the schools they went to. That's "real school," and they don't want anyone messing with it. This is true even among people who had a terrible time in school, which I liken to some bizarre variant of the Stockholm Syndrome, named after a famous bank robbery in Sweden, during which the hostages became emotionally attached to their captors and defended them upon their release.

Archaic mental models are holding us back when we can least afford delay. But, in my experience, the problems presented by these subconscious notions are exponentially exacerbated by the presence of a debilitating mental disease that I call "nostesia": fifty percent nostalgia, fifty percent amnesia. Simply put, nostesiacs are certain that the grand temples of learning that existed in their golden past were far superior to the dreadful schools we have today. Millions of Americans suffer from this delusion, and it is killing us as a nation.

I have encountered nostesia so many times that I've created an equation to quantify the severity of the affliction:

$$A \times O = NQ$$

A represents a person's age. O is number of years he or she has been out of school. Multiply these together and you get NQ—the

Chapter 11

Nostesia Quotient. The higher a person's NQ, the more advanced the disease. Anyone with an NQ over 1000 will struggle with the idea of change. Anyone with an NQ above 2000 is likely to be a pompous ideologue whose convictions about the glorious past degenerate into a torrent of defensive rhetoric when confronted with the facts. (Take my neighbor. Please.) There are mitigating and aggravating factors. If a person works in a school, or regularly volunteers in some meaningful capacity, then we can usually divide his or her NQ by two. If, on the other hand, a person is running for political office or works in higher education, then we can definitely multiply by ten.

One of my earliest exposures to nostesia came during a visit to western Nebraska. I was speaking to a community group at the invitation of the local superintendent. My talk was equal parts praise for the work of their educators and seminar on the need to change. In the Q&A that followed, a big fellow wearing a Stetson stood up and said, "You know, we're pretty conservative out here" (one of the top ten understatements of all time), "and as far as I'm concerned, if schools could just be the way they used to be, everything would be all right."

"Yes, sir," I said. "What year would that be?"

"Well, 1947. Those were pretty good schools."

"The dropout rate in Nebraska in the 1940s was over fifty percent," I said. "In fact, dropout counseling in those days consisted of principals encouraging some of the tougher kids to drop out. Today, your schools have that rate down to single or low double digits."

"Oh, that's not true," he shot back. "Everybody I graduated with graduated!"

Nostesia. Priceless.

At a public meeting in suburban Philadelphia, I introduced the 3Ts, and a woman said that none of the schools she attended used calculators and computers, and yet she and all her friends could count change *without* looking at the cash register. Proof positive that it used to be better.

In Phoenix, a retired machinist said that incorporating the discoveries of the cognitive revolution was unnecessary. His third grade teacher knew how kids learned. "Miss Hecker made us come up to the front of the class and do the times tables standing on one foot. And every time we stumbled she would whack us with her stick. That was real teaching!"

In meetings from Maine to California, men—always men—have told me, in no uncertain terms, that all my talk about school reform was bunk. "We just need to give them what I got. You know why? Because it was okay for me, and it'll be okay for these kids." Every time I hear the phrase, it takes a mighty act of will to keep from saying, "Sir. Isn't it obvious? It was *not* okay for you."

Nostesia is pandemic, and it has been for years:

1996. Educator E.D. Hirsch wrote *The Schools We Need and Why We Don't Have Them*, in which he called for a return to a traditional approach to education.

1994. IBM CEO Louis V. Gerstner proclaimed in *The New York Times* that "Our Schools Are Broken."

1983. *A Nation at Risk* warned of a rising tide of mediocrity.

1976. The Educational Testing Service presented college freshmen with forty-one multiple-choice questions on basic American history and found that they could correctly answer only half.

1969. Harvey B. Scribner, Chancellor of New York City schools, concluded that for every youngster who gained intellectually and psychologically, there was another who was, "pushed out, turned off, or scarred as a result of his school experience."

1963. Admiral Hyman Rickover published *American Education, a National Failure*. It became a national bestseller.

1959. With the launch of Sputnik, failing schools were identified as the reason the Russians beat us into space, prompting *LIFE* magazine to run an eight-part series entitled, "Crisis in Education," in which the editors wrote, "the standards of education are shockingly low."

1955. Best-selling author Rudolf Flesch wrote *Why Johnny Can't Read*.

1953. Historian Arthur Bestor wrote *Educational Wastelands: The Retreat from Learning in Our Public Schools*.

1942. *The New York Times* reported that only six percent of college freshmen could name the original thirteen colonies. One in four did not know who was president during the Civil War.

1940. The Navy tested its new pilots on their mastery of fourth grade math and found that sixty percent of high school graduates failed.

1939. Professor Mortimer J. Adler of Columbia University conducted studies in New Jersey and Pennsylvania, concluding that grade schools were devoid of discipline, high school students failed to master the basics, and college graduates could not read, write, or speak English well.

1933. The United States Office of Education found that teachers commonly promoted students they thought were failures.

1916. The first large-scale test of knowledge of United States history was administered. The results were abysmal.

1912. An eight-part series in the *Ladies Home Journal* concluded that schools failed to educate students.

1907. Woodrow Wilson said, "with all our teaching we train nobody...with all our instructing we educate nobody."

1892. Professor Joseph Mayer Rice visited schools in thirty-six cities where he found rote learning, mindless teaching, administrative ineptitude, political chicanery, and public apathy.

1889. Only the top three percent of America's students went to college, and yet 380 of 450 colleges reported the need for remedial courses in basic subjects for incoming freshmen.

1880. An essay by journalist Richard Grant White, "The Public School Failure," proclaimed that no institution had as much public confidence and pride and none was so unworthy.

1879. Harvard Professor A.S. Hill proclaimed that high school teachers were doing so little to teach young people to write that professors were forced to do the job.

For more than two hundred years, adults have claimed that the schools of their youth were superior in every way and that "these kids today" are academically deficient. And like their predecessors, today's nostesiacs have their own rationales. Some are convinced that schools were better "back in the day" because almost everybody got a job. They forget that most of those jobs—now gone—required little more than a strong back and a willingness to work. Some are alarmed because "these kids today" don't know the same things that they know, especially historical facts that they consider essential to being a good American. They forget that most of what they know now they learned *after* they got out of school. Some parrot the dreary assessment of our schools broadcast by media pundits they trust, and the only way they can change their position is to admit that they have been duped. A small number of nostesiacs are CAVE people: Citizens Against Virtually Everything. Facts are irrelevant to these folks. No amount of research or reasoned discourse will change their minds.

Mental models and nostesia separately and in toxic combination retard progress, but over the years I have learned that they are not the greatest obstacles to change. The greatest obstacle is deeper and more abstract: people resist changes that threaten to change their culture. And unfortunately, *everything* associated with our schools is connected to the culture of the surrounding town.

Chapter 11

My understanding of this cultural dynamic fully blossomed on a perfect spring night in southern Michigan as I sat in an auditorium that was overheated in more ways than one. Up to that point, I vaguely understood that even the most objective proposals were somehow tied to subjective concerns. I had repeatedly seen reforms rejected for reasons that seemed to have little to do with their merits. On this night, however, events conspired to present me with a moment of clarity.

It was my third visit to the district. The leaders there were planning major restructuring, including a revamp of the K-5 curriculum. After months of internal discussion and negotiation, a public meeting had been called as a forum to present their plans. I was not there in an official capacity. Earlier in the day at the superintendent's request I had given a talk to a combined meeting of the local service clubs. The topic was the importance of school/business partnerships in times of change. I had decided to spend the night to monitor the public event.

The crowd was small, as is usually the case for meetings at the school that have nothing to do with taxes or sports. It was quite warm. All the doors were wide open, and kids could be heard yelling and playing basketball in the gym. The meeting was going along just fine until someone in the audience came out of left field with a comment about whole language and phonics, and everyone froze. I had seen this before. In minutes, lines would be drawn, tempers would flare, and the opposing camps would talk past one another for the next two hours.

I was seated in the back of the room, ruing my decision to stay and unconsciously humming the theme song from M.A.S.H., when I had a vision. I suddenly saw the building not as a school, but as a concrete, external expression of an invisible cultural reality: a 3-D projection of the community's collective attitudes, values, and beliefs. All the hopes, opinions, and expectations of the people in the community and the people on staff were like genes combining to create the physical "body" of the school. It was as if a kind of cultural DNA sat at the center of everything. The school's architecture, curriculum, tests, texts, report cards, grade levels, bus routes, and extracurricular activities were all shaped by impulses of cultural information. Rules and regulations codified the community's shared expectations regarding when children first entered school, how long they attended, when their day started and stopped, when they were released for vacations, and what they had to do to graduate. Beyond pedagogy, more fundamental than any learning theory, I saw every aspect of the system springing from this invisible, all-powerful cultural core.

It was a peculiar vision, but if true, it explained so much. Above all, it meant that improving student achievement was not, primarily, a straightforward, objective undertaking where the normal rules of logic and reason applied. It was a subjective psychological and emotional endeavor that directly engaged, and often inflamed, the passions of everyone in the community. The leadership of every restructuring effort I had seen or been a part of had all but ignored this inner reality. No wonder we met such resistance.

I hated the whole idea.

I left the meeting and drove to my "deluxe" motel room on the edge of town. I finished off a cold pizza, got ready for bed, and spent the next five hours wrestling with wimpy pillows and scratchy sheets, the whole time drifting in and out of restless sleep and haunted by memories.

I recalled a packed school board meeting in Kentucky where some innocent soul, invoking Prichard Committee goals, floated the idea of school consolidation. It was like yelling "Fire!" in a crowded theater. Dozens of people began shouting that they were ready to go to war to keep their schools open. Their reasons had nothing to do with fiscal responsibility or student achievement, and everything to do with preserving cultural identity.

I found myself back in a contentious community meeting in Oregon where I had foolishly broached the subject of changing the district calendar. I was not entirely an idiot. I had made it abundantly clear that I was not recommending a move to year-round schools. I'd already discussed the Time Constant/Quality Variable problem, and I wondered aloud how long it would be before Americans realized that we couldn't adequately prepare our children to succeed in today's world by following a calendar used by our grandparents. I tried to soften the mood by pointing out that we accepted time as a variable in other learning endeavors. In scouting, for example, the boys and girls moved through their manuals at their own rate of speed, and no one was labeled "loser" if he or she took longer to earn a particular merit badge. I mentioned that flight school was open-ended; I had one friend who finished in four months and another who took five years before she successfully soloed the plane—I'm not flying with her, but she got her license. And I said that it was abundantly clear to me that time wasn't an issue in college—my darling son was in his fifth or sixth year with no end in sight.

"Only in the pursuit of a high school diploma" I said, "do we hold time constant, and woe to the child who fails to move up with his class; his chances of graduating dramatically decline, and, if he does graduate, he will be stigmatized as having been 'left back' for the rest of his life. How counterproductive is that?

"Why don't we change this? Why don't we make time a variable to ensure all our kids graduate having learned the things they need to know? Why don't we let go of a two-hundred-year-old system designed for the few, not the many? Why don't we restructure the schedule to help virtually every child actualize his or her full potential?"

As the last sentence left my mouth, a voice in the crowd cried out, "Who would play varsity?" And the floodgates opened.

"When would the buses run?"

"What about band practice and debate club?"

"What about piano lessons and cheerleaders?"

"What yearbook would they get?"

"What reunion class would they be part of?"

"What about Little League, and Bible school, and camp?"

"What about their jobs?"

"When would we take family vacations?"

"What about prom?"

I must have fallen asleep because there was a loud pop, and I awoke in the dark with "What about prom?" ringing in my head. It was 4:00 a.m. I sat up, and said out loud to the empty room a single, pregnant sentence:

> You cannot touch a school without touching the culture of the surrounding town.

This inescapable fact has since become my First Rule of School Restructuring. It is the most important thing that I have learned in the last twenty years.

No change takes place in isolation. Any attempt to significantly transform our schools alters the American way of life. A proposed change may be reasonable and necessary. Every child in the community might benefit. But its implications ripple far beyond the schoolhouse door. A change in the way we group kids changes social relationships among children and adults; a change in the schedule alters local traditions and disrupts established patterns of daily life. No matter where you touch a school, you touch the community in a very tender spot. We can base our plans on data and research, but from the community's perspective we are messing with their lives. We can invoke the prospect of raising achievement, but the community's innate cultural defense mechanism will perceive us as a threat that must be opposed.

Certainly there are people in every community who are willing to support the change process. They understand the stakes for their children and for themselves. They accept the need to restructure their schools even if it means making adjustments in their own lives. But when it comes to major change, there are usually not enough of these people to overcome the resistance. The record of school transformation over the last thirty years is replete with bloody battles, false starts, and abandoned initiatives because angry communities just said, "No!" The vast majority of Americans are not ready. And the prevalence of churning boards and shuffling superintendents tells me that legions of reformers have failed to grasp a basic truth.

My grudging acceptance of this truth eventually lead me to create my Second Rule of School Restructuring:

> To unfold the full potential of every child, we must do more than change our schools, we must change America one community at a time.

Daunting, but true. We must help the people of every community reconsider their relationship with their local schools. We must help them see that it is in their interest to capture the genius inherent in every profile of intelligence. We must help them realize that their schools as currently configured can no longer give them what they need. Only then will they be able to reimagine their schools and allow the changes that must take place.

My acceptance of these two rules was a watershed moment, and my understanding of their implications forced me to take a step back. It was not easy. People were finally listening to my message, and I felt tremendous pressure to push forward with the agenda. There was, however, no denying the fact that meaningful change would not, *could not,* occur in the face of community resistance. Getting the people who worked in our schools excited about the vision of possibilities was essential but not enough. We had to make sure that a significant cross-section of the community accepted the need for change before we could proceed. Another course correction was required. It was time to go to the community.

Chapter 12

Considering Community Involvement

*I am persuaded there is among the mass of our people
a fund of wisdom, integrity, and humanity which will
preserve their happiness in a tolerable measure.*

John Adams

T he change of focus did not come easily. A bit of a type A personality with a business background and, if my lovely wife is to be believed, possible control issues, I saw the path to improving student achievement in simple terms:

A ➤ ⟶ B

Establish the goal. Decide on a plan. Execute. The key issues surrounding our schools had been debated *ad nauseam*. We knew what we needed to do. Why retard the process by including a group of ill-informed, opinionated outsiders in a messy, protracted deliberation? Time was of the essence. Let's go!

The problem, of course, is that the people of the community are not outsiders. I was not dealing with a privately held corporation. When it comes to public education, everyone is a shareholder. They pay taxes. They have opinions, and they are all eligible to express their opinions at the ballot box. Going directly from **A** to **B** was not going to work in the public arena. There could be, and would be, temporary victories, but, in the long run, the status quo ante would prevail. A history teacher I met in Massachusetts said it best: "The community has the final word regarding the design of their schools, whether or not they come to any meetings."

To get from **A** to **B**, therefore, we were going to have to take the plunge into the community's cultural core, and we were going to have to go deep enough to influence the hearts and minds of the people who ultimately control our schools. We were going to have to address nostesia, mental models, and the attitudes and beliefs that hold the status quo in place. To get from **A** to **B**, we needed to go through **C.**

The question was, how?

At the time, the conventional wisdom held that increasing "community involvement" in our schools was essential to reducing tension, decreasing resistance, and strengthening support for district initiatives. Hundreds of education conferences featured community involvement workshops. Politicians promoted the concept in every speech. Professors extolled the virtues of community involvement, only they called it "the multidimensional interaction of interested persons representing a variety of disciplines and ways of knowing." Community involvement was included in 15,000 strategic plans. By the late 1990s, the term had become a national mantra. Only the word "paradigm" was used more.

I liked the idea, and I wanted it to be the answer, but I had grave reservations. It was true that my involvement had changed me, but mine was a unique case. I was paid to be involved, and my transformation had taken the concerted effort of many people over a period of years. Nothing I saw in the field led me to believe that my process could be replicated across an entire community.

First of all, very few districts had the time, the resources, or even the inclination to conduct a comprehensive community involvement campaign. Most teachers and administrators were already up to their eyeballs in work, and, truth be told, many had zero interest in engaging the public.

Second, in those few places where district leaders were eager, or, at least, willing to make the effort, the community's response was depressing. After months of focused effort, during which resources were committed, vertical teams were formed, and an aggressive campaign was launched to engage the public, the only people to respond were the same twelve parents and the one weirdo who came to all the meetings. If I saw this once, I saw it fifty times. I call it the "12 + 1" phenomenon.

To be fair, I attended some "kickoff" events that drew a much larger crowd. But regardless of the initial turnout, the involvement campaigns I saw ultimately produced the same anemic results: a lukewarm initial response, followed by the gradual loss of interest by the majority of participants. Six months after they started, all that remained were team leaders and a handful of loyal volunteers huddled alone in the auditorium on a Tuesday night with no reinforcements in sight.

For a while, I wondered if these districts were just going about it the wrong way. Maybe organizations working in other arenas were having more success involving the public in their cause. Everywhere I looked, however, I saw signs of less involvement, not more. Americans were joining fewer clubs, going to fewer community meetings, voting less, and socializing less. The connected, front-porch society of my youth was being replaced by a cloistered, back-deck society. We were drifting apart from one another and our communities, and we had been since the late 1960s.

The realization that the problem was universal was no comfort. Despite my reservations about the efficacy of involvement campaigns, I knew we needed to penetrate the community's cultural core, and I could think of no other way to do it. I concluded that we might be able to reverse the tide if we could determine why the public was pulling away, particularly from their schools. We could then tailor our actions to overcome the obstacles and increase involvement and support.

I was tempted, at first, to blame it on apathy. That was the general consensus: Americans talk a good game, but, when push comes to shove, they just don't care enough about their schools to get off their couches and act. There was, however, something cynically glib about this position. Maybe it was accurate, but I suspected that there were deeper forces afoot. I had learned so much from my audiences over the years that I decided to seek their help.

I was back to traveling constantly. There were years in the late 1990s and early 2000s when I spent more than a hundred and fifty days on the road. I was presenting variations of my talk, "Why Our Schools Need to Change," at in-service sessions, chamber of commerce lunches, school/business partnership dinners, foundation fundraisers, and scores of state, regional, and national conferences. Most of my talks were keynote presentations, but about a third were workshops, and it was in these that I began to pose the following question:

> We have never needed great schools more than we do today, and our schools have never had a greater need for public support. But what we find is that instead of coming closer, the public is drifting away. Why? What's going on in America to drive the public away

from their schools? Work together in your groups for fifteen minutes, and then we'll talk about what you've got.

The first time I asked, I knew I was on to something big. The room crackled with excitement. It was as if they were waiting to be asked. When it came time to report, their answers were insightful and profound. They examined the question from every conceivable angle. They cheered one another's replies. I left the session with an intuitive understanding that I had taken a big step closer to unraveling the riddle of **C**.

Over the next two years, I asked this question in every workshop. Tens of thousands of teachers, administrators, board members, classified employees, and community members sat together and developed their answers, and I am forever in their debt. At each stop, the number of answers grew, and I kept a running list. I soon realized, however, that most of the answers could be folded into twenty major social and economic trends that were shaping the culture of every American community. I am convinced these trends are wreaking havoc on the school/community relationship. They are driving substantial segments of the American people away from our schools just when we need them the most. I call them the Terrible Twenty Trends, and we must understand them if we are ever to get from **A** to **B.**

Chapter 13

The Terrible Twenty Trends

You don't need a weatherman to know
which way the wind blows.

Bob Dylan

T he Terrible Twenty Trends are described below in brief. (I have included an expanded description of each on my website.) They present a formidable challenge. I have seen auditoriums filled with the most seasoned professionals fall into a thoughtful silence when I present all twenty at once. I am convinced, however, that it is essential that we understand, or at least become familiar with these trends if we are to build the community support we need.

The trends are not listed in any order, with the exception of numbers one and two, which are invariably the first answers offered from coast to coast.

1. Changing Demographics. We are getting old. Less than 27% of adults have children in school. The graying of America is causing a fierce intergenerational competition for public funds. Priorities are changing, and there is a growing "been there, done that" attitude regarding support for local schools. Seniors are more concerned with health care, safety, and social security. And they vote!

2. Negative Media. If it bleeds it leads. America has few full-time education reporters. It takes time to understand education's complex issues. It takes time and space to explain the full implications of policy debates. Negative, sensational stories are easier to frame and report, and besides, they sell.

3. Fear of School Violence. Each horrific act of violence shakes the public. In truth, public schools are one of the safest places a child can be, but the perception of unsafe schools—reinforced by the media—frightens parents, increases public anxiety, and pushes the public away.

4. Culture War. Schools are ground zero in a war for control of America's future. Polarized worldviews collide in the classroom: one maintains that children are born good and can be helped to become better; one holds that children are innately bad and must be strictly disciplined to lead moral lives. The two sides battle over curriculum, instruction, assessment, and classroom management, and there is no room for accommodation. Regardless of who wins, public education loses support.

5. The Clanning of America. The melting pot is dead. For centuries, public education successfully served the motto, E Pluribus Unum. Now, E Pluribus Pluribus seems to be the goal. People go to great lengths to associate exclusively with others who share their ideas and beliefs. Parents declare, "We don't want our children to be with *them*. We want our kids to be with *us*." What was once a great strength of public education has become for some a cause for abandonment.

6. The Rights Revolution. We are awash in a sea of rights. Ever since education was proclaimed by the Supreme Court to be a property right, students and parents act from a dangerously overdeveloped sense of entitlement. The proliferation of rights has undermined the authority to manage students and perverted the "Holy Alliance": the all-important bond between teachers and parents. Collaboration and mutual respect have been replaced by confrontation and mistrust. The net effect is decreased public confidence in public education's ability to do the job.

7. The Rise of Special Interests. With liberty and justice for us! The number of organized advocacy groups has tripled in thirty years. These professionally staffed associations often act as though public schools were their private resource. They work to advance their members' private ends, and, in doing so, clash with educators who must consider the public good. The lose-lose results are predictable—guaranteed to both drain district resources and infuriate some segment of the public.

8. The Plague of Regulations. Nationally, the number of rules and regulations has exploded in a foolish and destructive search for legal perfection, and public education has been maimed in the process. Educators must comply even if the rules make no sense. Flexibility, judgment, and compromise have been muscled out of the equation. This infuriates parents who want results not red tape. They leave each futile encounter with the bureaucracy disappointed and angry.

9. Fear and Loathing of the Government. Our common institutions are the focus of a rising tide of ill will. Public schools are often a community's largest and most accessible government agencies, and, as such, they have become the focus of the free-floating antipathy of the left and the right. The usurpation of local control by state agencies, especially the unprecedented intrusion by feds, reinforces the public's belief that their schools neither listen nor act on their behalf.

10. The Frenzy of Privatization. We are in the midst of an ideological war waged against everything managed by government, including schools. Government operation is assumed to be inherently inferior to private management. Educators find the profit motive antithetical to their core mission, and many view the argument to privatize Pre-K-12 as the substitution of free-market rhetoric for rational thought. But this rhetoric resonates with concepts of freedom and choice that run deep in the American psyche. As long as proponents appeal to these currents, the crusade to privatize will undermine support for public schools.

11. Antitax Movement. No one likes paying taxes. Limiting taxes has been framed as both necessary and righteous, and proposition organizers contend that their actions are the quintessence of direct democracy. Frustrated community members who feel as though they have no voice in national debates seize upon public school bond elections as rare opportunities to be heard. They can vote "NO," and strike a blow against the government. Acrimony and resentment are inflamed each time a district asks for additional funds.

12. Schools as Scapegoats. No social or economic problem is too remote or too absurd to be attributed to inferior schools and lazy, self-serving educators. The constant blame game saps the energy and morale of the people who work within our schools, and undermines the commitment of the people who support them. Spurious accusations will continue as long as the public is lead to believe that schools are failing, and as long as finger-pointing grabs headlines and garners votes.

13. Union Bashing. The NEA and the AFT are lightning rods for criticism, and local schools suffer guilt by association. The unions have made powerful enemies in their attempts to promote public education and advance the interests of their members. Their defense of tenure infuriates many in business and rankles the general public. Top officials are accused of thwarting school improvement and subverting local control. These criticisms are used as a wedge to build resentment and drive the public away from their schools.

14. Public Perception of Alternatives. A growing number of Americans believe that there are many alternatives to public education, all superior. Promoters of various options reinforce this impression with sweeping, often unsubstantiated claims of success. Public confidence in the alternatives rises with each promotional salvo, producing a rationalized weakening of the traditional commitment to our schools. If public schools are perceived as one choice among many—and a crummy one at that—then the public has another reason to lose interest.

15. Demand for Customization. People are more demanding, knowledgeable, and empowered than ever before; they want everything "their way." Parents and students want schools to adjust to their specific needs. Public schools, however, were not designed to respond to individuals in such detail. The best they can do is evolve from mass-education to mass-customization, but only if Americans are willing to pay the substantial costs. Until then, resolute parents will collide with a one-size-fits-all system, and dissatisfaction will continue to grow.

16. International Comparisons. As a group, American students score no better than average on most international tests. Critics claim our "dismal" performance threatens our future. Educators label the tests flawed and misleading; they argue that comparing disaggregated results across diverse cultures is like comparing apples to guavas. Politicians and the press emphasize our position in the rankings as opposed to actual scores; they use tests as weapons instead of diagnostic tools. Each new wave of false comparisons gives the public another reason to turn away.

17. Standardized Testing. Never before have America's children taken so many standardized tests, and never before have they meant so much. Testing proponents, including many powerful political and corporate leaders, contend that standardized tests objectively quantify student performance as measured against rigorous standards. Critics argue that such testing is a meaningless pseudo-quantification of the learning process, telling us more about household income than student achievement. As long as the champions of testing can convince Americans that the tests are reliable, then the growth of this trend is assured. And as long as proficiency cut scores are arbitrarily set to ensure that millions of children fail, then this trend will continue to erode the public's faith in public schools, which some educators fear is the whole point.

18. Changing Job Market. Public education has historically afforded millions of young people access to the American dream, but the path of upward mobility has become more challenging. It is still true that those who graduate from high school earn more money than those who don't, but Americans of all educational levels face an economy with tougher entry requirements and greater insecurity. Uncertainty fosters fear, which breeds hostility directed at the schools. The gap between what schools provide and what the economy demands causes parents and taxpayers to question their continued support.

19. Ever-expanding Expectations. Americans now expect their schools to teach the basics, create responsible citizens, prepare effective workers, *and* respond to all the physical, emotional, and psychological needs of children living in a post-industrial society. It may be a laudable goal, but the bloated agenda disturbs many in the community. They intuitively understand that no institution can successfully be all things to all people. Seeing our schools make the attempt prompts them to reassess their commitment.

20. The Biloski Dilemma. I named this trend after the woman who introduced it. She was in the audience at a combined school/community workshop in western Pennsylvania. When it was her turn at the microphone she said, "I'll tell you what's pushing me away. It took me two days to find a baby-sitter so I could come to tonight's meeting. I'm working two jobs. So is my husband. I always want to be kept informed, but there is no way I can be any more involved. I'm just too busy." When she was finished, the audience broke into applause. She had struck a nerve. She was intelligent and motivated. She represented a fully employed, intact, nuclear family with kids in school. She cared enough about her kids and their schools to have rearranged her life to come to a meeting on a miserable night in March. And still, she could not be involved. Not because she was apathetic, not because she was ignorant, angry, lazy, or afraid, but because she and her husband and millions of people like them were dancing as fast as they could dance just to make their lives work. (I learned later that her name was Betty Jo Biloski. Everyone knew her as Nancy.)

℘℘

I was disheartened the first time I put all twenty trends together. Even my limited grasp of the implications of the social, economic, and political currents swirling through the general public was enough to make me realize we were sailing against the wind.

I was reminded of a video I'd seen years before featuring the cosmologist, Brian Swimme. The relevant section started with a reference to Ecclesiastes. Dr. Swimme maintained that there was a season for everything, and, cosmologically speaking, you could tell what season it was in the universe by looking at what was being created. He said, for example, that atoms did not form until eons after the Big Bang. The cosmos was just too hot to sustain their existence. At a precise point in the cooling process, however, it became "time for atoms," and they suddenly appeared in immeasurable abundance.

What made me think of this seemingly random reference was that Professor Swimme asserted that it would have been possible to create atoms earlier, but it would have required tremendous energy to overcome the background conditions, and, once formed, the atoms would have quickly disintegrated in the hostile environment. Oh brother! This described every community involvement process I had ever known. There had been victories along the way, but they had required tremendous energy, success was fleeting, and more times than not, the process demoralized everyone involved.

I was in a jam.

None of what I'd learned negated the fundamental truth: we needed a broad cross-section of community members to be with us before we could proceed to restructure our schools. I understood why so many people believed that increasing community involvement was the answer. It seemed so logical. But given the circumstances, I was hard-pressed to see how it was going to work. Of course, we could never stop trying to increase parental involvement, which is the greatest predictor of student success, but parents with school-aged children account for less than a third of the taxpaying public, not enough to overcome widespread resistance to change. We needed more than that.

My physicist father often told me that asking precisely the right question was the first step to solving a difficult problem—more than half the battle. As I reviewed my experiences, and considered everything I had learned and everything we needed to accomplish, gradually a simple question emerged: What do we absolutely need from the community? What do we need to be able to get from **A** to **B** so we can change the system and create rich learning environments that will help us unfold the full potential of every child?

Once I managed to clearly frame this question, the answers came in a rush.

Chapter 14

The Prerequisites of Progress

*The aim of the discussion, should
not be victory, but progress.*

Joseph Joubert

There are four things we need to get from **A** to **B**. I call them
the Prerequisites of Progress, and they build one upon another in a precise sequence.

Community Understanding

The first thing that we absolutely need is community understanding. The public will not buy a pig in a poke. Any attempt
to change the major building blocks of the system will threaten
beliefs, traditions, and assumptions that have controlled American thinking and behavior for generations. The community must
have a basic understanding of why change is necessary before
lasting, meaningful progress can take place.

The requisite understanding is built in layers. For each aspect
of the system we seek to restructure, the community must understand *what* we are doing now, *why* we do it that way, and *how*
we plan to change it. Members of the public must be told that
these changes will cause their schools to look and feel different;
they will no longer conform to the memories and models of "real
school" they have in their heads.

Every member of the community must also understand the extensive array of benefits that restructuring their schools will afford. In other words, the people must fully grasp what's in it for them *whether or not they have children in school*. Self-interest may not always trump altruism, but that's the way to bet.

Most of all, everyone in the community must understand that they are depressing their local economy, undermining the health of their neighborhoods, and spoiling their quality of life by maintaining the selecting system. Doggedly clinging to the industrial model or fantasizing about the schools of the past will not produce the results they want and need no matter how hard their educators work. The system they know was not designed to prepare children for the twenty-first century. Waiting to change it is indefensible. The public must understand that the time for change has come.

Increasing community (and staff) understanding is the first Prerequisite of Progress. Any attempt to change a school that ignores this step almost always leads to disaster.

Community Trust

Second, we need community trust. I cannot overstate the importance of trust in the context of improving our schools. It is not enough for the public to understand and accept the need for change. Restructuring a system that took decades to build cannot occur without high levels of mutual trust. If we are serious about creating schools that unfold the full potential of every child, then changes are coming that few people fully comprehend—certainly not I. Schools are complex organisms with lots of moving parts. Mistakes will be made. Money will be needed. Emotions will run hot. The community must trust its educators to do the job.

There was a time when high levels of public trust were a given. My parents and most parents on my street trusted my teachers and our principal, Mr. Tropea. (We didn't! Only Charles Dickens would surrender innocent five-year-olds to a tall, scary man with a black mustache, a glass eye, and a wooden leg. He trolled the halls like Ahab!) Unfortunately, much of that essential trust is gone, eroded by the Terrible Twenty, and as we shall see, by the foolish, thoughtless, and, sometimes, self-destructive actions of educators. We need to deliberately rebuild that trust. The people must know that their educators are not just trying to "feather their own nests" or "experiment on our kids." They must trust that their educators are on their side—partners working *for* the community, not aloof professionals who happen to work *in* the community.

Fortunately, community understanding engenders community trust. The more understanding we cultivate, the more the public will trust that we have the vision, energy, and expertise to succeed.

Community (and staff) trust is the second Prerequisite of Progress. It is the lubricant that keeps the process moving forward during difficult times.

Community Permission

Third, we need community permission. In many ways, the need for permission lies at the heart of this book. As my First Rule of School Restructuring states, you cannot touch a school without touching the culture of the town. Many of us have learned the hard way that proposing even modest changes can incite a riot. Once, in suburban Chicago, I saw three hundred angry parents screaming with veins popping out of their foreheads over a proposal to introduce block scheduling at the high school.

When the stakes are so high and the potential for backlash so great, we must, to the greatest extent possible, secure the community's permission to proceed. We need a green light. The signal may be as concrete as a "Yes" vote in a bond election, or as abstract as a tacit nod—a "sense of the community"—that becomes obvious only by listening carefully to the various ways that the community talks to itself.

Fortunately, permission is a byproduct of understanding and trust. Once we have increased understanding of the issues, and after we have established a heightened level of trust, it is more likely that a critical mass of community members will permit the process to evolve.

Community (and staff) permission is the third Prerequisite of Progress. Without it, the record of abandoned initiatives will continue to grow.

Community Support

Finally, we need community support. If I know anything, it is that schools cannot do it alone. Those who work in public education cannot fulfill society's enormous collection of academic and social demands by themselves. There are teachers and administrators who believe they can, but they're deluded. If the public expects our schools to develop the post-industrial basics in every child—basics like literacy, numeracy, thinking and teamwork skills, self-discipline, knowledge of the world, knowledge of self, and the capacity for lifelong learning—then the people of the community must act as partners. They must demonstrate patience, respect, appreciation, generosity, and, eventually, active participation in the creation of a vibrant learning environment throughout the entire community.

Securing community support is the fourth Prerequisite of Progress. It ensures that our friends, family, and neighbors begin to act as owners of their schools.

Understanding, trust, permission, and support. These are the precious resources contained within **C** that we absolutely must have to get from **A** to **B**. This is what we need to make changes and make them stick. Armed with these four, we dramatically increase our chances of creating schools that unfold the full potential of every child.

෨෬

The clarity that came with the answers was wonderful. I felt as though I had drilled down to bedrock, and was finally standing on solid ground. Now, all I had to do was figure out what course of action would deliver the goods.

Whatever it was, it had to be theoretically appealing and tactically sound: something that would produce positive results throughout the entire community in spite of the fact that most districts had little in the way of time, resources, or inclination to engage the public. The action steps had to capitalize on public education's many strengths; they had to be appealing and accessible enough to encourage the participation of *everyone* in every district regardless of his or her workload, official role, or responsibility. A viable pursuit of the Prerequisites of Progress also had to account for the twenty social and economic trends that were flowing fast against us. In short, whatever we tried to do to secure understanding, trust, permission, and support, it had to be practical, powerful, and above all, doable at the local level.

Which finally brings us to The Great Conversation.

PART IV

The Great Conversation

Chapter 15

Escaping the Status Quo

Public sentiment is everything. With public sentiment,
nothing can fail; without it nothing can succeed.

Abraham Lincoln

The Great Conversation is a positive, ongoing discussion between educators and the people of the communities they serve. The action steps take us deep enough into the fabric of the community to challenge nostesia, reshape mental models, and counter the effects of the Terrible Twenty Trends.

The process is neither complex nor costly. It adds little to the existing burden. *No new money or personnel are required.* It can be successfully executed in any district, not just those favored by history, geography, or economics. It is not like so many programs that assume everyone magically possesses the extra time, know-how, and materials they need to succeed. Anyone interested in participating in this process already has everything he or she needs to be effective. Properly executed, The Great Conversation informs, inspires, and invigorates all who choose to participate.

It is my strongest recommendation that The Great Conversation become an integral part of any effort to restructure our schools. This is the central proposal of this book. Everything I have learned since joining the Roundtable has convinced me that this position is correct. The course of human events has carried us to a moment of great opportunity. Unfolding the full potential of every child is no longer an impractical, utopian fantasy. It's our nation's greatest need. The education that America's best parents have always wanted for their children is now a necessity for all children. We must use The Great Conversation to marshal our considerable resources and create a grand culture of student achievement. We must do this in every community. And we must do it now.

I know this conclusion makes many educators squirm. They have talked enough. I empathize. Each year, too many children leave our schools unprepared to thrive and prosper as adults. The best interests of our children, our communities, and our country demand that we move as fast as we can to create schools that maximize student success.

The problem is we can't. Americans are not ready. Attempting even small changes can rile local sensibilities. Undertaking major reforms without securing the Prerequisites of Progress can trigger open revolt. Educators are trapped in a maddening series of events that unfold in a never-ending loop:

> A sensational incident (think Sputnik) or a critical "blue ribbon" report on test scores triggers public alarm. All at once, politicians, business leaders, academicians, and journalists clamor for reform in speeches and articles that are verbatim recreations of critiques written five, ten, twenty, fifty years before. A new wave of laws and regulations spawns the next big thing in instruction; their programs may or may not increase student achievement, but someone in the private sector always gets rich. Teachers and administrators respond by charging once again into the breach: organizing, planning, attending conferences, adjusting the curriculum, and creating lesson plans. New ideas collide with established traditions as programs are implemented. "That ain't the way we do it around here!" becomes the rallying cry of reac-

tionaries on staff and in the surrounding community. Ancient grievances are awakened that have nothing to do with either the best interests of kids or the matters at hand. Tempers flare. Cynicism grows. The battle is joined. A new Board is elected. A new superintendent is hired who is guaranteed not to rock the boat. And somewhere deep in the background, the enemies of public education snicker, and the relentless machinery of the selecting and sorting system grinds on utterly unfazed by the tumult, churning out results we no longer want or need.

I've watched this bizarre existential play for two decades. Many who read these pages have labored as prisoners of the cast for much longer; they have no control over the script, but they are repeatedly condemned for their performance. This show must *not* go on.

The Great Conversation is no panacea, but it can help break the cycle. Each step is designed to promote a meaningful flow of two-way communication that sets the stage for progress. In my most optimistic moments, I fancy that The Great Conversation can change America; it can usher in a new dawn of public vitality where the continuous education of every American, young and old, is the centerpiece of a vibrant, participatory democracy. But whether or not it can launch a national learning revolution, I know for sure that this positive discussion is powerful enough to help every district escape the mental, emotional, and cultural grip of the status quo.

The Great Conversation is easy to understand and execute. The process is built to run on two tracks. One formal. One informal. The formal track is a deliberate, organized, *group action* that targets the entire community. The centerpiece of the formal track is a scripted message that evolves over time in a series of distinct phases. Usually, this track is initiated and maintained at the district level, but it can be launched by a school or a cluster of neighboring schools.

The informal track is comprised of hundreds of casual discussions conducted by *individuals* talking to family, friends, and acquaintances within the course of their daily routines. The informal track has no formal script, but it becomes much more potent when private conversations echo, at least in part, the message that is being circulated in the formal track.

The two tracks are synergistic. Pursued together they quickly produce the outcomes we seek plus an impressive array of secondary benefits. They are not, however, dependent. Each track can run in isolation. Each yields its own practical results.

Participation in either or both tracks is *completely voluntary*. This is important. Teachers and administrators are already awash in mandates and directives. No one should be bullied or forced to join. Having said that, participation in the Conversation should not be left to the superintendent and a committee of the usual volunteers. Everyone in the district has a vested interest in the outcome, and everyone should play a part. The potential benefits far outweigh the time and energy invested, and broad participation ensures maximum results.

The mechanics of The Great Conversation are described at length in the "how to" chapters that follow. There is, however, a personnel issue that must first be addressed. It concerns leadership.

As mentioned above, The Great Conversation can be successfully initiated and maintained in any community. Progress can be made even in the most challenging circumstances once someone has made the conscious choice to begin. The question is, who makes this choice? Who leads?

The answer depends upon local circumstances, but anyone can lead.

My preference is for members of the district's leadership and governance team to manage the process. They have legitimate power, and, in most communities, an unrivaled capacity for outreach across social and institutional boundaries. They are the most knowledgeable actors in the change process, and, as we shall see, it will be their staff members who deliver the message in the formal track. Whether or not they lead, however, senior administrators, teacher-leaders, and board members must, at a minimum, approve of and support the process. If they are indifferent or hostile, the chances of conducting a successful Conversation are nil.

In those situations where the district's leaders support the Conversation but, for whatever reason, are unable to lead, there are many other qualified candidates.

First among them, in my biased opinion, are the leaders of local chambers of commerce and economic development councils. In concert with educators, business leaders are natural allies in the development of human capital. Few groups have a greater vested interest in increasing student success, and many already partner with their schools. At the very least, they and their employees must be encouraged to join the Conversation and do whatever they can to facilitate the dispersion of the district's message. My only caveat to having business leaders pilot the process is that they must be mindful to act as collaborators, not rogue elephants. Changing our schools is a much slower, much more nettlesome process than any private sector restructuring. Frustration here is a fact of life. It's okay to press for progress, but business leaders must step back every now and then, take a deep breath, and guard against the tendency to become overbearing bullies claiming to have all the answers. That approach is counterproductive. (Been there, done that.)

Educational Service Centers (ESCs) can also lead. I am a big fan of Intermediate Units, AEAs, CESAs, BOCESs, and Regional Offices. Most are very close to the districts they serve and familiar with the local communities. They are in a unique position to bring disparate players into the process. Some have the resources and personnel needed to sustain the Conversation over time regardless of leadership changes within the districts—a crucial contribution. The ESCs also have a powerful incentive to participate: their actions enhance their perceived value among their member districts *and* among critical members of their state legislatures.

Parents and parent groups are candidates for leadership. My two-year tenure on the board of the National PTA brought me face-to-face with the tremendous commitment and organizing power of this outstanding group, especially members of the local affiliates. I suppose I should not have been surprised since my mother was president of our PTA for years, and I never met a better organizer than Mom. Every parent brings energy and authenticity to the process, and some have the passion, status, and skills to build a powerful community-wide network of volunteers.

The leaders of local education foundations (LEFs) can also initiate and maintain the Conversation. Many of these influential organizations are already deeply involved in raising awareness of the need to increase student success. Their members are organized, motivated, and embedded in the community. As their numbers and budgets grow, LEFs are positioned to play an increasingly significant role in the formal track.

Representatives from higher education can lead The Great Conversation, provided that a) they become full partners, i.e., they resist the temptation to treat the process as a research project and the people on staff as guinea pigs, and b) they can sustain their commitment over time.

Officers and faculty from local community and technical colleges may also lead. These educators strategically bridge the worlds of school and work, and, in some areas of the country, they are integral parts of the communities they serve. They can be effective leaders as long as they can avoid exacerbating turf wars between themselves, the four-year institutions, and ECSs.

Finally, it is possible for a single, motivated individual to lead.

A local champion with the proper energy and skills could instigate a chain of human interactions that would lead to success in both the formal and informal tracks.

Regardless of who leads, it is very, very important that, *prior to taking the lead*, he, she, or they have good relations with the people working within their schools. And I'm not just referring to the possible leaders who may be outsiders. I have seen administrators and board members *assume* that they have a close relationship with their staffs. This would be nice, but it is not always the case, and the assumption can lead to big trouble. I have tremendous respect for teachers—I am routinely humbled by their courage, compassion, and expertise—but let's face it, they can be a touchy bunch. They will refuse to participate if they are suspicious of the leaders' motivations. Worse, they'll strangle The Great Conversation in the cradle if they conclude that it's just one more top-down, central office mandate that has been developed without giving the slightest thought to their opinion, their workload, or professional expertise. (Been there, done that too.)

I have one final thought on leadership. This is no place for the control freaks among us to attempt to exert our will. Once begun, The Great Conversation becomes an organic discussion among adults embedded within an evolving network of relationships. The interpersonal dynamics are too complex to control. In this endeavor, leaders serve best when they create an environment that energizes the collective intelligence and encourages broad participation.

With the above observations in mind, we are ready to proceed to the mechanics. The action steps described are conceptually simple and easy to execute. They are, above all, *doable*: rooted in reality; built on the basis of what districts can actually do with existing resources and personnel. Each step is designed to produce maximum rewards, with minimal effort. I start with the formal track.

Chapter 16

The Formal Track

*What you have to do and the way you have
to do it is incredibly simple. Whether you are
willing to do it, that's another matter.*

Peter Drucker

The formal track of The Great Conversation is a positive, organized group activity designed to engage educators and
the public in an ongoing discussion about increasing student success.

The structure is simple. Once begun, the formal track unfolds
in a series of phases, each featuring a new piece of the district's
message. I favor launching two phases per year, fall and spring,
but there is no perfect schedule, and even partial execution yields
substantial benefits. Phases will vary in length: a phase will be
considered complete only after its distinct message has been
shared throughout the community. It is possible that successive
phases will overlap. This is not a problem.

Organizing the formal track into phases affords two procedur-
al advantages. First, it allows us to divide our message into easily
presentable, easily digestible bits. Second, it makes it easy to keep
track of our progress.

The most important feature of the formal track is that it takes
place on the **community's turf** at the **community's convenience**.

This must be understood: we are going to them. This stands in sharp contrast to the traditional approach to public engagement, which too often revolves around meetings and activities held in the evening at the school. *Maybe* asking the community to come to us made sense years ago when the pace of change was slow and most people had kids in school. But today, with demographic realignment, rapid social restructuring, and the erosion of public trust, attempting to engage the community on our turf at our convenience just doesn't cut it. We must go to them.

This shift in venue provides six major benefits.

1. By going to them, we greatly expand the size of our audience. The number of people who hear our message is no longer diminished by conflicts with competing community activities, sporting events, or primetime TV. It is not reduced by disinterest, forgetfulness, fatigue, or discomfort with the setting. This last point is key. There are hundreds of grown-ups in every community who are scared to death of school, and many more who carry a grudge: they had horrible experiences inside the selecting system when they were kids, and, years later, it still gives them the willies just to smell the place. Choosing the school as the venue may be logistically sound, but the site acts as a filter that suppresses turnout. It all but guarantees that only certain kinds of people will attend.

The proof of this assertion is clear in the factual record. Districts everywhere go to great lengths to invite the people of their communities to "important meetings" held at the school. They send letters home with the kids. They put announcements in the district newsletter. The superintendent writes an article for the local paper. The meeting is promoted on the radio, details are publicized on the district's website and cable channel, and an e-mail campaign is launched. Handwritten notes are sent to VIPs, and posters blanket the town. All this and more is done to encourage attendance. And if the meeting has nothing to do with raising taxes, downsizing the sports program, or choosing cheerleaders—and if there is no free food—who shows up?

That's right, 12 + 1: the same twelve parents and the one weirdo who comes to all the meetings. This hardly qualifies as a robust conversation.

The trends of time demand that we engage a much bigger audience. By shifting the venue, by sharing our message on the community's turf at the community's convenience, we get the audience we need.

2. By shifting the venue, we increase audience receptivity. People listen and respond differently when they are sitting among their peers in a safe, familiar environment. Comfort levels are up. Defensive shields are down. This combination of factors greatly improves the chances that more of our message will be heard, absorbed, and remembered.

3. Our audiences are better behaved on their turf. Peer groups tend to police their own. They moderate the contentious or boorish behavior of their members, especially when they are on a tight schedule. I think of this as a classroom management issue, and it's a big deal in my experience.

Numerous times, I've sat in meetings held at the school and watched a community member—let's call him Frank—go on and on about some real or perceived problem that has nothing to do with the evening's presentation. On the surface, it might appear that we would have more control of the situation in "our house." But the dynamics are not in our favor. We invited Frank to join us. He inconvenienced himself to come to our meeting. He invested his time and energy. He has been explicitly or implicitly asked for input, and, by golly, he's going to give it. Whether he is a parent or not is irrelevant; he's a taxpayer. The poor presenter has little choice but to stand and listen with a fixed expression of interest on her face as her stomach acids slowly rise and dissolve the lining of her esophagus. Meanwhile, as the clock ticks away, the rest of the people in the auditorium squirm in their seats, ruing their decision to attend, and praying for someone to put them out of their misery.

Change the venue, however, and the dynamic shifts. Frank is now surrounded by his peers and bound by the rules of behavior established by the group. Their meetings follow a concise routine. They have places to go, and they are eager to get on with the show. If Frank goes on too long, they have the standing and the inclination to say something that we could never say: "Frank, sit down and shut up."

Shifting the venue will not eliminate extraneous comments or questions. And, as we shall see, courtesy requires that we always take a quick moment to acknowledge the feedback and promise a personal response following the event. But when we are in "their house," even without their help, we can control the situation by referencing the group's desire to end on time. In one stroke, we demonstrate our respect for their busy schedule, and we keep the audience focused on our message. It's a big win-win.

4. The time constraints imposed by most meetings in the community force us to sharpen our message. We have to tailor our remarks to ensure that we finish within the allotted time. This is especially important for presenters who are more predisposed to talk than listen—a not uncommon trait among teachers.

5. By moving the Conversation to the community's turf we change perceptions of "us" and "them." Teachers and administrators get out of their buildings to see and be seen. They learn more about the people, the organizations, and the businesses surrounding their schools. On the other hand, community members get to see and speak with educators beyond the usual representatives of senior management. Knowledge and familiarity grow among parties. This is especially valuable in those districts where many members of the staff—sometimes as much as eighty percent—either choose or are forced by finances to live outside the

community.

6. The sixth and final benefit is huge: by shifting the venue, we can easily and precisely monitor the diffusion of our message throughout the community. Taking our show on the road enables us to create a tracking system that provides a precise record of where we have been and what has been said. We can quantify the size and composition of each audience, and we can record their response. Conversely, at any point in the process, we can see where we have yet to go: we can see the geographic and demographic holes in our coverage area, and we can plan our next steps accordingly.

Together, the benefits that accrue when we take our message to the community's turf are priceless. We dramatically increase the size of our audience; we gain greater control over the flow of our information; we enjoy positive changes in the audience, the message, and the messengers. By making the effort to meet the people where and when it's convenient for them to meet— where there is no fear or resentment, and where everyone feels welcome—we set the stage for a discussion that is more relaxed, authentic, and productive. We no longer have to hope (pray) that the people will come to us. We go to them. In doing this, we ensure greater exposure to and acceptance of our message.

In order to effectively take this step, however, we must create a map.

Chapter 17

Mapping the Community

Americans of all ages, all conditions, and all dispositions, constantly form associations.... I have often admired the extreme skill with which the inhabitants of the United States succeed in proposing a common object to the exertions of a great many men, and in getting them voluntarily to pursue it....

Alexis de Tocqueville

A functional map of the community's turf is made up of groups and categories, and it can be created in an hour. The mapping process is easiest and most enjoyable when done in a workshop format. I have worked with as few as five people and as many as four hundred, and each time they produced an excellent map. My favorite sessions include the entire district staff—certified and classified—and any volunteers from the community who want to play a part. In those districts where the staff may not reflect the diversity of the surrounding community, it is wise to cast a wider net by inviting members of underrepresented constituencies to participate.

Mapping the community's turf has little to do with defining physical boundaries. We already know the geography. We are interested in mapping people, and we are generally more interested in groups than individuals.

In most communities, there is no shortage of groups. As de Tocqueville observed, Americans love to join together for common purpose. In 2010, there were 2,380 charterd groups with national affiliates, including the Grand Order of the Antelopes, the National Association for Outlaw and Lawman History, and, of course, the Elvis Presley Burning Love Fan Club.

Our goal in the mapping session is threefold:

1. Identify all the groups that regularly or periodically gather in the community

2. Determine when and where they meet, and

3. Organize them into the categories described below.

There are a number of ways to accomplish this. I have seen easels placed around the room holding newsprint pads, each displaying a single category heading, e.g., Civic Clubs. The assembled mapmakers individually move from station to station adding their ideas to the list. I have also been in settings where participants were divided into teams, and each team was given a list of all the categories and asked to create a map. Facilitators merged the lists at the end of the session to create a master map. Both methods have their merits, and I'm sure there are other ways to accomplish the task, but no matter how it's done, our goal is to tap the collective knowledge of all the participants. Many will be members of one or more groups, and those who are not will know others who are. Chamber of Commerce directories, business registries, municipal and county fact books, and area phone books can, and should, be consulted to spur creative thinking and create more thorough lists.

Describing the process in this way suggests a level of orderliness that may not exist in a typical mapping session. They can be quite animated. New categories may emerge as the groups are identified, and some groups may be overlooked. That's okay. Precision is not required. As long as we finish the session with a reasonably comprehensive list of the community's groups appropriately placed in general categories, the mapping is a success. There will be ample opportunities to fill in the blanks.

The number of categories will vary with the size and complexity of the community. I have worked in some small districts where all the groups could be listed on a single page. Even here, there is much to be gained by completing the mapping exercise. In most communities, I recommend starting by creating a separate category for each of the groups below. The first six are obvious.

1. Civic clubs and organizations

2. Fraternal societies

3. Professional associations

4. Labor and farm organizations

5. Ethnic societies

6. Businesses over a certain size (how big depends on the community)

The remaining seven need some explanation.

7. All local religious institutions

I have watched audience members become uncomfortable when I suggest including religious groups in The Great Conversation's formal track. The cultural tensions that surround issues of church and state have become so great that the notion of public schools actively engaging these groups strikes some as inappropriate, if not illegal. Neither is true.

I rarely admit that I'm a lawyer because it never does me any good. (I worked for years in the happy land of ice cream to remove the taint.) I no longer practice law, but I have retained an interest in cases related to the separation of church and state, particularly as they relate to schools. I can safely report that *nowhere* has the Supreme Court said that educators and the clergy can never talk about student success or the future of public schools. Based on the current levels of interaction between the two groups one would think that such a prohibition exists. It's a shame.

In my work with districts and their communities, I have often gone out of my way to meet with the local Ministerial Alliance. The ensuing discussions are always lively, thoughtful, and productive. Many, many times, however, the religious leaders have told me that they have rarely, if ever, been included in discussions regarding the direction of their local schools even though they have been preaching in the community for years.

This experience suggests that we don't have a "bright line" of separation between church and state as required by the Constitution. We have an iron curtain. And it's killing us as a nation. Historically, families, churches, and schools worked in concert to educate the children of the community. I know that changes in our society have altered the dynamics among these three institutions, but their active cooperation is still greatly needed if we are serious about increasing student success.

By making the point that we must go to them, I am not suggesting that we cede control of school policy or curriculum to local clergy. That *is* out of bounds. But these men and women are genuinely concerned about the children of the community, and genuinely concerned with the quality of their local schools. They are also powerful opinion leaders. By aggressively including members of the clergy in The Great Conversation, we raise understanding and trust among the members of an important constituency, and we help them discuss school-related issues with their parishioners.

I know that there are some preachers in every community who are focused inward—more interested in the development of their congregations and less interested in engaging with public schools. Some are openly hostile. We should always invite them into our discussions, even those who treat public schools with open disdain. Fortunately, they are a minority. Most of the religious leaders are open to dialogue. Many, if not all, are in the midst of their own institutional restructuring, and they are grappling with the same issues and obstacles facing our schools; they understand what it means to have someone tell them, "That ain't the way we do it 'round here." We can benefit from their experience and guidance.

It is also worth noting that many of their congregants are predisposed to join us in our efforts to build a community-wide culture of student achievement. Active involvement in a religious organization is *the* strongest predictor of both philanthropy and volunteering. Churchgoers are substantially more likely to be involved in secular organizations like schools than other members of the public. And the connections run both ways: public school teachers represent nearly half of all the Sunday school teachers in America. We engage one of the greatest repositories of social capital in America by including religious institutions in our map.

Finally, I want to make it clear that I am not recommending that we take the formal track to church, synagogue, mosque, or meetinghouse during formal services. There are other options. The bulletin board in my church contains announcements for the Career Builders workshop, Middle East Crisis study series, and the Men and Women Who Love Too Much Support Group to name a few. Addressing these particular groups may or may not be appropriate, but the point is that there are plenty of opportunities to present our message to members within a congregation apart from their devotional activities, and we create allies when we do.

The groups in categories 8 – 10 have an extraordinarily close relationship with our schools. Each has a vested interest in the success of The Great Conversation, and all are predisposed to listen to and actively disseminate our message.

8. Internal groups

This category includes all the groups formed and operating inside our schools. These include first and foremost the certified and classified staffs, plus PTAs, site councils, and advisory committees. I have witnessed a marked tendency on the part of administrators and board members to overlook these groups in their eagerness to engage the public. For example, they assume their employees are already interested and involved in The Great Conversation and, therefore, need no special attention. Big mistake. These people are powerful. They are often the largest employee group in the community, many have vast social networks, and all are de facto ambassadors of the district. It just makes good sense to keep them fully informed. The staff also represents the premier source of highly qualified potential participants, either as presenters in the formal track, casual contributors in the informal track, or both. We want to entice them to join us, and we serve that end by keeping them in the loop. At the very least, we must treat everyone on the inside with the respect we accord all the other groups on our list. Not only because it's right, but because these folks will strangle The Great Conversation in the cradle if they feel as though they've been ignored.

9. Existing partners

This category is comprised of all the external groups who partner with schools on a periodic or ongoing basis, e.g., social service agencies, government departments, city councils, county commissions, citizen advisory groups, foundations, business boards, and boosters. The main point of this book is that schools cannot unfold the full potential of every child alone. We need all the help we can get. We increase the likelihood that these groups will join us in creating a community-wide culture of student achievement when we make sure to include them in the formal track.

10. Vendors

This category is made up of organizations selling anything to our schools. They have an obvious, vested interest in helping us advance our cause. We shouldn't feel shy about asking them to join the effort.

11. Miscellaneous groups

This category is made up of groups that are less formal and, perhaps, less organized. Such groups include:

> Book clubs
> Seniors' groups
> Retired employee groups
> Historical societies
> Boards of realtors
> Homeowners associations
> Academic societies
> Women's groups
> Men's groups
> Athletic associations
> Travel clubs
> Home/school councils
> Various fraternities and sororities
> Student groups
> Garden clubs
> Toastmaster clubs

12. Ad Hoc assemblies

This category is unlike any listed above. It's comprised of groups of people who are temporarily, and loosely, joined together in common purpose. These groups include many people who will appear nowhere else on our lists—people we would otherwise miss. Examples of such groups include crowds at sporting events, shoppers in malls, people in libraries, patrons of eating and drinking establishments, people in barber shops, hair salons, gymnasiums, theaters, galleries, grocery stores, lumberyards, laundromats, swimming pools, and visitors to community centers. The activities that bring these groups together rarely afford opportunities to make formal presentations, but they do offer us opportunities to present exhibits or sound bites that reinforce our message. This is especially true for those events that take place on our turf, such as student performances, art shows, and all sporting events. I am not suggesting that we make a speech at halftime on Friday night, but we can find creative ways to make a positive impression on each captive audience.

13. Virtual communities

As the horizontal world of web-based networks explodes, we need a separate category for all the virtual "communities of interest" that gather on social media sites such as Facebook, Twitter, LinkedIn, and the district's websites and message boards. I would include in this category a group of relevant local bloggers.

Once all the categories are determined and all the groups identified and categorized, the information can be saved and regularly updated in any number of print or electronic formats. From a promotional perspective, however, and to help all interested parties keep track of our progress, it's wise to create a visual representation of our map and post it in a prominent place. The display need be no more than a series of 30"x40" posters, each with a category name at the top and four columns underneath.

Civic Clubs and Organizations

Group	Phase #1	Phase #2	Phase #3
Rotary Red Lion Restaurant Noon every Friday Drew D'Angelo, Pres. 216-324-1825 48 members	04-21-2010 **Success Overview** Presenting: Meehan, Miller, Burke, Zipper. *Good response* *Need more examples*	09-15-2010 **21st Century Skills** Presenting: Giannetta, Swanson, Morris, Dumont. *Great interest, some disbelief.*	03-12-2011 **Bond Election** Development Committee plus Ciccone. *Lots of questions* *General support*
Lions meeting place meeting time contact phone number members			
Kiwanis meeting place meeting time contact phone number members			

The groups assigned to each category are placed on the left in the first column. Ideally, each entry in column one contains the name of the group, the time and location of its meetings, the number of members, and the name and phone number of the designated contact. The miscellaneous groups may not have formal schedules or permanent locations, but the name of the contact will suffice. The ad hoc category will contain a list of venues and a schedule of their planned activities. The virtual category will list URLs.

Columns two, three, and four are used to monitor our progress as the formal track unfolds, one column for each phase. (New posters are added over time.) Pertinent information is recorded in these columns each time a presentation to a group is completed. Ideally, this tracking data will include the date of the presentation, the topic presented, the names of the presenters, and the number of people in attendance. Specific, albeit, cryptic comments regarding audience feedback can be added.

Once the posters have been created, they can be mounted side by side to create a map of the community's turf that is easy to comprehend. To enhance the impact of the poster array, I recommend adding a large copy of the district's geographical map marked with stickers to identify the location of each meeting site. (Those of us who are a tad obsessive can color code the stickers according to their category.) Each time one of our teams makes a presentation in the formal track, we record it on the poster and place a pushpin on the map at the corresponding site. It's also enlightening to have everyone on staff place a pin showing where he or she lives. People living outside the district can place their pins on the border closest to their homes.

Presenting a poster array like this in a highly visible location affords three benefits: it graphically reinforces the idea of the community's turf; any interested party can, with just a glance, easily see where we have been and where we still need to go; and it gives a satisfying sense of progress to fully engaged participants and casual observers alike. We "find" our community by identifying and categorizing all our local groups. But we "see" our community with the help of this display.

There is one more piece of the mapping that must be accomplished before we can move to the next step, but this category we do not display.

I mentioned above that we are generally more interested in identifying groups than individuals. The formal track of the Conversation is a wholesale, not a retail, operation. As a young man, I worked as a regional coordinator for the American Cancer Society, and I witnessed the tremendous power of a house-to-house awareness campaign. But only in my wildest dreams do I see the formal track as a one-on-one activity. I used the word *generally*, however, because there are important exceptions to the rule.

Within every community there are certain individuals who deserve special attention. These "movers and shakers" can accelerate, broaden, and deepen The Great Conversation by virtue of their occupation, their social position, or their personality. I emphasize that this category should not be displayed because, years ago, I learned the hard way that it's a mistake to post a list of these people for all to see; some on the list will be mortified, and others, who failed to make the cut, will be outraged. We improve our chances of success when we include these individuals in our target audience. But we keep this list to ourselves.

The first category of influential individuals is made up of those who deserve special attention because of their occupation or position. This list includes elected officials, prominent business leaders, certain policymakers and government employees, select academicians, judges and judicial officers, journalists, realtors, and some TV and radio personalities. (I assume that most officers of the PTA will be active participants in the formal track, but if they are not, they should be included here.) The men and women in these positions are often quite influential among their peers and in the wider community. Our efforts to increase student success are well served when we make a special effort to keep them informed.

The second category of individuals worthy of special attention is made up of those community members who possess certain personality traits. The people in this group may have no official rank or position, but they can help quickly spread our message simply on the basis of who they are. Malcolm Gladwell in his book *The Tipping Point* divides these people into three categories: connectors, mavens, and salesmen.

Connectors connect people to people. They know a lot of people and they are always befriending more. They have a special gift for bringing people together. My friend Harry fits the description. I have no idea how Harry ever gets anything done. He is constantly talking to other people, most of whom he hardly knows. Pass him on the street and he will introduce you to whomever he's with. Many of his relationships are what sociologists call "weak ties," acquaintances as opposed to deep friendships, but he has hundreds of them with all kinds of folks, and he moves effortlessly among them, bridging and connecting all the way. From the perspective of the formal track, Harry is very powerful. The more people like him who understand and endorse our goals, the more quickly our message will travel across the community, and the more compelling it will become.

Mavens expose people to new ideas. They love accumulating new knowledge and sharing what they know. They are not braggarts. They genuinely want to help, and, because of this, others look to them as credible, nonbiased sources of advice. I offer my brother-in-law Carl as Exhibit A. Want to buy TiVo? Carl will thoroughly review the entire digital video recorder industry and tell you where to shop for the best price. Want to find the best place to dine in Philadelphia? You are going to hear about everything from cheese steaks in South Philly to the menu at Le Bec-Fin. By singling out mavens like Carl and providing them with the main points of our evolving message, we greatly advance our cause.

When Gladwell speaks of salesmen, he is not talking about people who happen to work in sales. He means natural salesmen. For reasons unknown, these people are far more "emotionally contagious" than the average person. They exhibit an easy charm and an air of authority within their area of expertise. They possess an uncanny ability to persuade. We have all met at least one, and have probably bought whatever they were selling. The more natural salesmen we identify, the stronger The Great Conversation will be.

There is one final group of individuals who merit special attention, although I am never sure what to call them. Describing this group brings to mind the sage advice of the great philosopher, Don Corleone, of *Godfather* fame: "Keep your friends close. Keep your enemies closer." In every community there is a core of individuals who resist whatever we are trying to accomplish: they oppose our schools, and our plans; they resist the idea of change in general. I have seen a tendency on the part of some change agents to ignore them, which I understand because they are usually unpleasant. We must, however, be sure to keep them informed. I want to make it perfectly clear that I am not suggesting that we waste valuable time and precious energy trying to convince these peddlers of negativity that they are wrong and we are right. That's a mistake. Only a masochist allows himself to become deliberately entangled in their infuriating, circular arguments that, by their very nature, offer no hope of resolution. Arguing and pleading with these people—I call them Retros—is a waste. They will not change. It's genetic. In spite of this, however, it's smart to keep them informed. Offer them the same steady stream of information that is being presented to everyone else in the formal track. Promote the positive. Do not hide the negative.

If we do this, it will be harder—though not impossible—for them to claim that The Great Conversation is just the latest piece in the grand conspiracy.

೫ೞ

Turf mapping is an ongoing process. The universe of groups will change over time. Movers and shakers will come and go. Our maps will, and should, evolve. But a concerted effort to identify and categorize all groups at the outset of the formal track will provide every district with a valuable map of the community's turf. It costs nothing but some time, and the map can be put to use as soon as we are ready to launch.

This brings us to the next step. Once we have identified our target audiences and where they can be found, we must decide what we want to say.

Chapter 18

Deciding on the Message

*I know no safe depository of the ultimate powers of
the society but the people themselves; and if we think
them not enlightened enough to exercise their control
with a wholesome discretion, the remedy is not to
take it from them but to inform their discretion.*

Thomas Jefferson

What are we going to say?

This is *the* question for many who hear my talks. All eyes
snap to the front when I broach the subject. Everyone leans in.
The silence in the room deepens. Even the teacher in the last row
who has been grading papers since she sat down looks up and
waits. The need for The Great Conversation may be great, the
process may be important, but it's what we say to the public that
defines us. The message must make sense; it must be something
we can embrace. I know very few people who willingly promote a
message they don't endorse, and all of them are lawyers.

I'm happy to offer my answer to the big question, but with the
following caveats. First, no third-party recommendations should
be adopted wholesale, including mine. The most compelling part
of any message will always include facts and stories drawn from
personal experiences. To the greatest extent possible, my suggestions, if used at all, must be adapted to reflect local conditions.

Second, there is no perfect message, and searching for one will retard progress. Our objective is to move the people of our community along a continuum: from ignorance and suspicion to understanding and trust; from rejection and indifference to permission and support. The truth is that almost any message can, and will, facilitate this movement if it clearly explains the reasons that schools and communities must increase student success.

Third, the message should not be confrontational. Years of experience have taught me that there is widespread confusion on this point. Frustrated teachers have approached me with tales of idiot neighbors who blather on about the failure of public schools. "I'm tired of being put on the defensive by these clowns who spew mindless dogma and statistics out of context. You want me to participate in this conversation of yours? Fine. But only if you give me the facts and figures I need to shut them up."

I empathize, but the reasoning is flawed. Many of the offending gasbags could care less about the facts, no matter how artfully presented. What's more, victory over the nasty and the ignorant is not our goal. It may feel good to bludgeon some belligerent boob with a brilliant defense. (Okay, it does feel good.) But administering a good beat-down is not going to convert critics into allies, nor will it win their support in raising student achievement. And that *is* the goal. We win by gaining public support. We triumph by building cooperative relationships based upon shared interests and mutual respect. Whatever we put in our message, it must help cultivate these relationships.

In my experience, if we are to create these essential relationships, the message we share with the community must contain four basic themes:

1. We must give the people concrete, practical reasons to feel good about their schools. This is no time to be shy. We must constantly promote our success in all its forms. Discussing our achievements must be our default position.

2. We must continually explain the urgent need for change. In every phase of the formal track, we must tell the public why we must unfold the full potential of every child and why our schools must change if we are achieve this goal.

3. It is crucial that we help every member of the community understand what he or she can personally gain from the creation of great schools. They must understand what's in it for them. Every person we address must understand that his or her quality of life is directly tied to the quality of the local schools. Most Americans do not see this big picture, and they will not rally to our aid unless we help them connect the dots.

4. We must make it clear from the outset that we seek an open, honest exchange of information and ideas. This commitment to robust feedback must be genuine. Americans are suspicious of hype, for good reason. They will quickly tune out and turn off if they suspect that The Great Conversation is a public relations charade. It's okay if the commitment to a frank, two-way dialogue is tentative at first. Past encounters with members of the public have left many teachers and administrators feeling as though they were mugged. But as long as we start with good intentions and remain consistent in our efforts to listen and connect, eventually, all parties will lower their shields, and the cooperative relationships we need will begin to grow.

Promoting our success, explaining the need for change, making it personal, and remaining steadfast in our desire to connect. Developing these themes is essential to our long-term success. They must be reinforced in every presentation.

With these provisions in mind, I offer an introductory message in seven parts, plus Q&A.

Part 1. Welcome

Thank the organizers for the opportunity to speak, and immediately welcome the entire audience to the beginning of The

Great Conversation, "a new community-wide discussion, designed to increase student success, and, ultimately, improve the quality of life of everyone in the community, whether or not they have kids in school." Introduce the members of the team—who they are and what they do—and state that they are all volunteers. Explain that this presentation is the first in an ongoing series, and that similar presentations will take place across the district in the weeks and months to come. This declaration reinforces the impression that something new has begun; a train is moving, and everyone is on board.

Emphasize that The Great Conversation is intended to be a dialogue, not a monologue. "Each time we appear before you, we will have something important to share about our schools, our students, and how they relate to you and the future of our community, but we need to know what you think." This declaration is important. Right or wrong, many people in the community feel as though their opinions have been either carelessly overlooked or intentionally ignored. Some who hear our message will doubt our sincerity. So be it. By stating our purpose, we have set the stage to prove them wrong.

Explain that The Great Conversation will proceed in a series of phases, and in Phase One the objective is threefold: to connect with as many people as possible; to describe the benefits that will flow if we work together to increase student achievement; and to help everyone understand what these benefits will mean for the community. "It is our hope that this understanding will inspire the growth of a community-wide culture of learning that supports student success, *and* leads to a new era of security and prosperity for all of us."

State up front that The Great Conversation is not about fundraising. We need never be shy about the importance of money, but we should make it plain that fundraising is not our purpose. This is very important. Over the last few decades, many districts have developed a terrible habit of reaching out to "engage" the community only when they need more cash. Not surprisingly, Americans have become jaded; they reflexively hide their wallets when they see us coming. There is no doubt there will be times when a district will need to raise revenue. And I am very happy to report that a wonderful byproduct of the formal track is a significant increase in the number of "Yes" votes on school bond election night. I have seen it repeatedly. But fundraising per se is not what this endeavor is about, and we score points with the community when we reach out to them without asking for money. If the district's need for new funds is imminent, I advise postponing the launch of the formal track until the development campaign is complete. Keep the two efforts separate. "In this presentation, we seek only two contributions: your attention and your feedback."

Three things are accomplished by opening the formal track in this way: we state our broad intentions; we pique everyone's self-interest; and, if we do a good job, we arouse the desire that all human beings share to be part of something great, something bigger than ourselves.

Part 2. Explain the timing

"We are coming to you now because a fundamental transformation is taking place in America, and no one is exempt. The future of everyone in this community is tied to the quality of our schools as never before. The industrial age we grew up in is fading. The knowledge age is taking its place. No one can accurately predict what jobs will be created in the next twenty years—too much is happening much too fast—but it's clear the success of the American economy depends less on making and moving *things*, and more on generating and sharing *knowledge*. This shift has triggered a dramatic increase in what our students need to know when they graduate. What was considered an adequate education just thirty years ago is no longer sufficient."

State clearly that this is especially true for the majority of young people in the community who will not go to college. "In the past, these kids entered fields or factories, mills or mines, or a million small shops; they were part of the great mass of unskilled or semiskilled workers who held jobs that paid them a decent wage their entire lives. They didn't need a high-quality education to get these jobs. Not too long ago, they didn't even need a diploma. They needed to show up on time, work hard, and do what they were told. Seventy-seven percent of the American labor force fit this description as late as the 1970s. Now, low-skilled workers account for less than twelve percent of the jobs paying a decent wage, and that number is falling rapidly. Gone are the days when a marginally educated kid could leave school with a strong back and a willingness to work and catch the American Dream."

It is important to make the case that most jobs worth having today require *more than* a high school diploma. Many people don't know this. Emphasize that every student must graduate, and every graduate must demonstrate that he or she has learned the traditional basics—the 3Rs—*plus* the new basics—the 3Ts: thinking, technology, and teamwork skills. "To make it in the workplace today, entry level workers must have the skills to constantly learn new things, and they must be able to apply what they have learned to a continuously changing stream of occupational problems and personal challenges. For the first time in American history, every student needs a high-quality education, not just the kids at the top of the class."

Underline the need to prepare *all* kids to succeed. It is a nice notion in the abstract, but the truth is that most people are primarily interested in ensuring the success of their own kids. Acknowledge that this is natural, but emphasize that changes in American society, especially the economy, demand that we consider the interests of every child in our community. "Our quality of life is affected by these kids, whether we know them or not.

Crime rates, health services, tax revenues, civic participation, the strength of the local economy, and quality of our local government will all improve with higher levels of student success. We can't force someone else's child to learn, but it's in everyone's interest to come together to encourage success and remove the barriers to achievement. It's not only the right thing to do, it's practical."

Part 3. Share good news

Every presentation should feature a few concrete examples of progress and success: stories of student achievement, news of a staff member's professional advancement, an announcement of a district milestone, news of awards or grants. Every step of progress, big or small, is worthy of discussion, but it's best to lead with examples of student achievement. They can come from classwork, homework, extracurricular activities, and tests. These accounts of good news are akin to injections of a powerful antibiotic, specially formulated to combat the virulent strains of cynicism that sicken the public psyche.

I continually encounter resistance to my call to promote success. People, especially teachers, have told me, "Jamie, we're not that good at tooting our own horns." My response is simple: it's time to learn. News of our achievements is the most inspiring information we have to share, and, miraculously, it's exactly what the public most wants to hear. Americans hunger for signs that schools promote the traditional values of persistence, discipline and hard work. They want to know that their schools are effective, safe and orderly. They want to know that their schools strive to develop productive citizens who are prepared to take care of themselves and contribute to their society. By taking time to share solid evidence of progress in every presentation, we assure the people of our community that their trust *and their money* are not misplaced.

Fortunately, we have a great story to tell. Anyone who says that there's little success to report is either grossly misinformed or a liar. I have been in rich, gleaming, state-of-the-art public schools that are lighthouses of learning and world-class incubators of creativity. Here, the success is palpable. I have been in poor, decaying buildings where the staffs labor with limited resources to serve children who are overwhelmed by all the dark forces that postmodern America can muster. These schools are local tragedies and a national embarrassment. But, even here, miracles occur every day. They are not all the sunbeams-streaming-through-the-clouds, angels-singing-in-the-heavens kind of miracles, although I suspect that on some level they are. Most are quiet breakthroughs, small victories, steps of student understanding and insight. When we couple these miracles with concrete examples of student effort, a compelling story of achievement unfolds.

I cannot draw upon this wealth of daily experience to build my message. I've heard many accounts of progress over the years from excited staff, and I've been fortunate to be visiting the right class at the right time to witness magical moments, but I remain an outsider. What I have built is a narrative that tells the story of public education's astonishing success. My talking points include:

• A historical review of the direct connection between the expansion of public education and the wondrous, unprecedented, uninterrupted rise in the educational attainment of the American people over the last hundred years.

• An examination of the increase in academic rigor within public schools over the last three decades, including the increase in both the number and difficulty of classes offered, and the trends in the amount of work assigned.

• The steady rise of standardized test scores as seen in the NAEP and SAT/ACT.

• America's remarkable showing on international tests of student achievement as evidenced by *disaggregated* scores on the

TIMSS, PISA, and PIRLS, including a review of why these tests should be approached with caution.

• The increase in the number of high school graduates and the growth of college enrollment over the last fifty years.

• The increase in college graduation rates among men and women across all racial and ethnic groups, including a marked increase in numbers receiving master's and doctorate degrees.

• The profound, positive change in the educational profile of the American public as reflected in a broad spectrum of cultural indicators, including the huge number of books published and purchased, rising museum attendance, and ticket sales to classical music events.

• Statistics regarding school safety, all of which show—headlines notwithstanding—that America's schools are safe and they make their communities safer.

Taken together, these points demonstrate that America's public schools have produced the best-educated population in the history.[6]

"Every day, our schools encourage levels of innovation, risk-taking, and exploration that are the envy of educators around the world. Despite all the poverty and social challenges facing our public schools, each year they release the creative genius of millions of young Americans. Since their creation over two hundred years ago, public schools have enlarged the wealth and vitality of our people, and played a central role in making the United States the world's preeminent power. Public education is the principal mechanism through which America makes good on her fundamental promises of liberty, justice, and opportunity for all.

"And our schools have done all this while feeding tens of millions of children nutritious meals twice a day, transporting them billions of miles each year in safe, reliable buses, and providing them with quality health services and medical expertise at little

---

[6] The full text can be found at www.jamievollmer.com.

or no cost. If that were not enough, America's public schools are the cultural heart of their communities. In an era of waning social capital, our schools provide hundreds of thousands of opportunities for families, friends, neighbors and strangers to come together and enjoy sporting events, music recitals, plays, art exhibits, dances, and scholastic competitions."

Public education's record of achievement is spectacular by any measure, and, teacher reticence aside, we must do everything we can to make this plain to everyone we speak with in the formal track.

Part 4. Introduce the topic of school restructuring

This is not an issue that can be dealt with in a single presentation, but we must broach the subject.

The need to tap the full potential of every child has already been addressed in Part 2, but everyone in the audience must understand that their schools were never designed to accomplish this task. They were created by the nation's founders to select and sort students into two groups, thinkers and doers, according to the needs of an agrarian society. Over two hundred years later, the basic building blocks of the system remain intact.

"No matter what your views on the global economy, low-skill/high wage jobs are a thing of the past. If we are serious about preparing *all* children to succeed in the twenty-first century, then our schools must change. We can't keep doing the same thing we've always done and expect to get a different result. The time has come to replace the rigid selecting and sorting process with a flexible approach to teaching and learning that is designed to produce one result: student success. We cannot accomplish this goal without making significant changes in the way we group kids, the way we teach and test them, the school schedule, and the school calendar. However, if educators have learned anything in the last twenty years, it's that changing schools cannot be done without the understanding, trust, permission, and support of the public. Knowing this, in the months to come, we want to talk with you more about the changes our schools need to make to increase student success, why these changes are important, and what they will mean for everyone in the community."

Remind the audience that their feedback in this process will be vital. As an opening exercise, ask them to start thinking about what they think the children of the community should know and be able to do when they graduate.

Part 5. Schools cannot do it alone

No introduction to The Great Conversation can be considered complete without making it clear that schools need the help of the entire community.

For all of public education's remarkable success, no generation of educators in the history of the world has been asked to do what Americans now demand of their schools. Few members of the community understand this. Most have almost no idea of the burden that has been placed upon their schools. They left the classroom when they were teenagers. Few have ever been back. Seventy percent have no school-age children. For most Americans, the challenge of teaching is out-of-sight, out-of-mind.

The easiest *and fastest* way I know to bring them up to speed is to read aloud from the poster, "The Ever-Increasing Burden on America's Public Schools." The presentation of this information has a stunning impact. I have never given a speech without reading some or all of the list. As I roll through the decades, it becomes clear to even the harshest critic that their schools cannot possibly fulfill such a sweeping mandate alone; they are going to need the support of everyone in the room. In case someone was sleeping during the reading, I recommend that each person in the audience be given a hard copy of the list when they leave.

Part 6. Finish with one "amazing fact"

Amazing facts are school-related statistics that educators may take for granted, but that the public is likely to find extraordinary. These items have the potential to make a deep impression because most people have no idea of what really goes on in their schools, even though most are convinced they do.

One category of amazing facts includes those that reveal the scope of routine activity, the more specific the better. For example, the number of meals served in a week; better yet, how many pounds of flour, tomatoes, or cheese are consumed. Other facts include: the number of extracurricular activities that take place in a year and what they cost; the number of students who transfer in and out of the district each year; how many pages of bureaucratic forms are filed per week. My personal favorite is how much money the kindergarten teacher would make if she were paid the same amount that an *average* daycare provider charges for the same number of hours for the same number of kids ($680/child/ month x 9 months x 25 children = $153,000). Compare this number to her actual salary.

Another category of amazing facts is related to tests. Handing out a recent test helps the audience see what the kids are learning in school, and it's usually a revelation. The kind of test doesn't matter, but middle school math tests are always a devilish choice. Distribute a copy of the test to everyone, but do not make the people take the exam on the spot unless you are feeling particularly cruel. The failure rate would be colossal, and embarrassing the audience is not the goal. Let them take the tests home as food for thought. It may cause them to think twice before complaining about "these kids today."

The most fun category of amazing facts includes those that refute nostesia: the notion that schools used to be better. One of the current hot button issues among nostesiacs is the "outrageous" number of today's college freshmen who need remediation in basic subjects. This subject receives a tremendous amount of media attention, and it's often offered as proof positive of failing schools. (Headlines say little about why U.S. colleges are accepting all these kids if they are so deficient, but that's another story.)

A perfect example of this rhetoric is found in a quote that appeared in the *Los Angeles Times* attributed to Professor Theodore M. Greene of Princeton University. On page 2, under the headline, "High-School Failure Decried," the professor said:

> I know of no college or university in the country that doesn't have to offer most or all of its freshmen courses in remedial English, beginning mathematics, beginning science and beginning foreign languages. Consequently, we give two or three years of college [courses] and the rest is high school work. Progressive education went too far.

What's amazing about this fact is that Professor Greene made this statement on March 26, 1946. What's just as amazing is that thirty-eight years earlier, in 1908, a Carnegie report revealed that forty-nine percent of freshmen entering *Ivy League* schools were admitted with "conditions," a code word for "in need of remediation." Even further back, in 1900, eighty-four percent of America's colleges reported that incoming freshman needed remedial work. This occurred at a time when only the top *two percent* of high school graduates were accepted to college, compared to *sixty-two percent* today.

The amazing fact exercise could be considered optional, but, if added, it should take no more than a few minutes to complete. It gets the people in the room thinking differently about their schools, and, in the case of the nostesiacs, it helps to break the futile habit of looking back to a mythical golden era of education for answers to the complex problems facing our schools today.

Part 7. Q&A

This is not optional. The formal track will only work if its presenters both talk *and* listen. The public will reject the process if it appears to be no more than a public relations campaign, or a disguised attempt to gain public approval for decisions that have already been made. We must facilitate open dialogue if we are serious about nurturing cooperative relationships, and a dialogue is not a series of monologues delivered in the presence of witnesses. We must offer balanced, objective information *and* we must provide bona fide opportunities for people to respond with their questions, opinions, and insights.

Encouraging feedback may be intimidating at first, but the district has much to gain in the process. We accelerate the growth of public trust, and we tap the collective wisdom of the community when we hear all sides. By encouraging dialogue, we are more likely to expose any biases that may be coloring our thinking *before* they cause major problems. This is especially true in districts where the staff does not reflect the diversity of the surrounding community.

Concluding each presentation with a Q&A session is an essential element of the strategy to increase student success. It will help to counter the Terrible Twenty Trends and move the public from resistance to support, and it will become increasingly important as The Great Conversation evolves.

೫০೦෪

I chose to offer these specific suggestions for Phase One because I have seen them work. Sharing good news helps community members see their schools for what they are: engines of growth and opportunity. Raising the issue of timing gets people thinking about the social and economic changes they see around them and how they affect their schools. More importantly, it helps members of the public begin to connect the dots between their quality of life and the quality of their schools. Explaining the problems associated with the selecting system puts everyone on notice that things can't stay the same. Reading the never-ending list of mandates accentuates the need for community support. Sharing amazing facts promotes discussion across backyard fences and at the dinner table.

These points have been field-tested, but whether or not a district chooses to incorporate any of my suggestions must depend upon the answer to a single question: will discussing these ideas help you strengthen your relationships with the community and increase understanding, trust, permission and support? Any ideas that accomplish this objective can be used to create an effective message.

Once there is general agreement on what we are going to say, we must organize the content to ensure that we deliver a coherent presentation. This necessitates the creation of simple scripts.

Chapter 19

Developing Scripts

Who speaks, sows. Who listens, reaps.

Argentine Proverb

To a large degree, the development of scripts is what makes the formal track formal. Winging it is not an option. The stakes are too high. After we have decided upon what we want to say, we must carefully consider how we plan to say it before we hit the road.

There are six principal advantages to developing and using scripts:

1. They help presenters stay on message.

2. They provide support and confidence to presenters.

3. They help presenters define their responsibilities.

4. They expose everyone in the community and on staff to the same message at approximately the same time.

5. They provide all staff members—whether or not they choose to become involved in the formal track—with an understanding of the message, which helps them to answer questions that arise from family, friends, and neighbors.

6. They provide a written record of what's been said as The Great Conversation evolves.

Scripts are powerful management tools, but there is no perfect script. They can be elaborate or lean, with or without visuals.

Most are more than talking points and less than essays, but any format will serve as long as the presenters are comfortable.

There are, however, three rules that must be obeyed. First, the script must allow the presenters to deliver the entire message within the allotted period of time. Second, the scripts should never assume that the audience has prior knowledge of the topic. Third, they must be scrupulously stripped of jargon.

There are also three guidelines: the best scripts should be flexible enough to accommodate variations in style, precise enough to discourage emotional presenters—a.k.a. loose cannons—from flying off the topic, and clear enough to be understood by a lay audience. And, of course, they must be designed to encourage audience feedback.

The total time allotted for our presentations will be fixed by the schedules of the groups we address. How much time we build into the script for Q&A will vary with the setting. In some cases, a few minutes at the end of the presentation will be all the schedule allows. This isn't a problem if we follow some simple steps. First, answer each question as quickly as possible, resisting tangents and eschewing in-depth analyses when a succinct answer will suffice. Second, efficiently deal with questions that, for any reason, cannot be answered immediately by writing them down and promising a speedy answer. ("We'll have to get back to you" is an acceptable response if no one knows the answer.) Third, if the meeting ends before all questions are answered, apologize, provide an e-mail address or phone number, and encourage those who want more information to make contact. In regard to steps two and three, I strongly recommend that someone from the district respond to each questioner in a timely manner, i.e., within two days. This is essential if we want to demonstrate that we are serious about increasing trust, and the extra effort is usually greatly appreciated.

Once a script is composed, the teams of presenters must decide among themselves how to divide the content. Most presentations made on the community's turf will be short, usually falling some-where between seventeen and thirty-five minutes. No one will be required to speak for more than a few minutes if each presenter delivers a few main points. Sharing the responsibility in this way lightens everyone's load, and, from the audience's perspective, variations in style, physique, voice, and personality add inter-est and increase attention. In dividing the script, the presenters should consider experiences or anecdotes they might have that might complement any or all parts of the message. Personalizing the script in this way can add immediacy and power to the pre-sentation, as long as it can be done within the allotted time.

The last step in the scripting process is very important. Once the scripts have been finalized and reviewed by senior manage-ment (this is no place for surprises), everyone on staff must be given a copy. Sharing the scripts internally is both the right thing to do and the smart thing to do. It's the right thing to do because it ensures that every employee knows *in advance* what is being formally presented to the community. When it comes to commu-nicating with the public, too often members of the professional and support staffs are left in the dark. They hear about what the district is saying after the fact, usually from family and friends. This can be embarrassing, especially when the news comes from their know-it-all Uncle Bob. If we fail to share the script inter-nally, we increase the chances that discomfited staff members will undermine the entire process.

Keeping the staff in the loop is also the smart thing to do be-cause it promotes buy-in and participation. Sharing information builds a sense of ownership even among those who initially choose not to participate. It helps keep everyone focused. It also keeps everyone more or less on the same page. Finally, exposing every-one to the message awakens the collective wisdom of the staff and encourages the bubbling up of practical ideas for improvement.

Developing scripts, like mapping, is an action step that is doable by any group. It requires some time but no money, and the time invested pays dividends throughout the life of the formal track. Talking points become sharper and more refined. Ideas are presented in a logical and sequential flow. The scripts prepared for successive phases provide a written record of our progress as the message evolves.

Of course, once we have scripted our message, we need presenters.

Chapter 20

Building Teams

Let us work together for unity and love.

Mahatma Gandhi

D on't send anyone out there alone. This is one of the cardinal rules of the formal track: teams of two to four presenters should carry the message to the community. Almost any group of reasonable people can form an effective team, but I recommend teams composed primarily of teachers and members of the classified staff. Of course, supportive community members are welcome, and students can be included in special circumstances. Administrators and board members, however, should refrain from being presenters. They can, and should, actively participate in the development, implementation, and management of each phase, but in the context of The Great Conversation their appearance before the public should be limited.

I promote this particular team configuration not because I'm in awe of teachers, although I am, but because I'm eager to give The Great Conversation every tactical advantage, and polls consistently show that Americans trust teachers more than they trust administrators or board members. (These last two groups always score better than lawyers, but that is probably cold comfort.) Teachers love it when I inform them of their exalted status. They puff up with pride, and their chests swell right until I drop the other shoe: Americans trust bus drivers, custodians, and school secretaries more than they trust teachers. After all, these folks know where all the bodies are buried.

My experience is consistent with these polls. I have observed audiences in scores of public meetings, and there is no doubt that their reactions differ depending on the presenters. People are always polite when administrators speak, but when teachers take the stage, a change in body language occurs; the group becomes more focused. The same increase in attention is apparent when support staff and community volunteers deliver the message. I cannot prove that the different responses are a function of increased confidence or trust. It may be that community members have become accustomed to having administrators and board members speak for the schools, and they are simply reacting to the novelty of a new group. But whatever the reason, audience receptivity grows and our message becomes more memorable when we change the messengers.

Of course, not every teacher is thrilled by the prospect of speaking to members of the community. I have seen their smiles of pride quickly replaced by dark looks of misgiving, if not stark terror, when my recommendation that teachers take the lead sinks in. Even some of the people who want to help are unnerved by the thought of standing before the public. Each time I see it, I am reminded of a teacher who approached me after a speech in Florida. "Okay," she said, "you've convinced me that this thing is important not only to my students but to me, and I would like to play a role. But I could never go out there and talk to a group like the Rotary. I'm not qualified. I'm just a teacher."

For the record, I hate the phrase, "just a teacher." But I let it pass, and said, "You know, I hear that a lot. Do you mind my asking what you teach?"

"I teach ninth grade history," she said. "Twenty-three years."

"Let me get this straight," I said. "You stand in front of rooms filled with surly ninth graders all day, and you are afraid to talk to the Rotary? Ma'am, they're just fat, bald ninth graders. Trust me, you'll recognize them when you walk into the room."

Having said that, I understood her misgivings and the hesitancy of the many people just like her. Their anxiety most often springs from three concerns.

First, as the lady suggested, prospective team members worry that they are not qualified to effectively present the material. Of course, this is why we take the time to develop scripts. Concise, coherent scripts ensure that each team member has the tools he or she needs to effectively deliver the message. Eloquence is great, but it's not required to be an effective presenter. The formal track would never get off the ground if everyone had to be Abe Lincoln. Clear, jargon-free delivery will suffice.

Second, candidates worry that they won't be able answer all the questions that might arise. As we learned in the previous chapter, however, no one will ever be expected to have all the answers to all the questions that our presentations inspire. We answer the questions we can and defer answering those we cannot, always assuring the questioner that an answer will follow soon. And, to belabor the point, we must make good on that promise *in a timely manner.*

The third source of speaker apprehension is related to classroom management: presenters fear that they will be unable to control an audience member who becomes unruly during a presentation. As stated earlier, however, both the venue and the nature of the audience work in our favor. Audience members are usually on a tight schedule and they are among equals. They are never shy to cut off a peer who gets out of line. I concede that there's always the potential for an individual to become a complete jerk, but the established group dynamics make it unlikely that the unpleasantness will spin out of control. In fact, the only time in twenty years that I saw a person rant and rave despite their protesting peers, the sentiment of the audience swung so wildly in favor of the team of teachers that I was tempted to tip the guy ten bucks as a token of my appreciation.

The truth is that no one need fear joining a team. The scripts and the division of labor they promote, plus the advantages we enjoy by shifting the venue from our house to theirs, combine to make the task easy and enjoyable. Everyone in the district can participate. And the benefits of understanding, trust, permission, and support would come in a glorious flood if they did.

But they won't.

I have been encouraging active involvement in the formal track for a long time. Long enough to know that, even among people who are excited about The Great Conversation, many will pass on being a presenter no matter what I say. Some would rather crawl through broken glass than speak in front of an audience. Others believe that their strengths lie elsewhere. The good news for each group is that there are many rewarding, accessible avenues of participation that do not entail gong before the public. Most districts have at their disposal a wealth of communication tools that can be strategically employed, without added cost, to reinforce the work of the presenting teams. Established communication instruments offer opportunities for everyone to play an active role in the process, and, in doing so, broaden and deepen our reach. The next step in the formal track is identifying these tools.

Chapter 21

Conducting a Communications Audit

There's something about what happens when we talk.

Lucinda Williams

The easiest way to identify the district's communication tools is to conduct an audit. List all the ways the district communicates with the public, directly and indirectly. Inventories are likely to include:

Websites—fast, straightforward, high quality, up-to-date
Social media networks—YouTube, Facebook, Twitter
In-house blogs with anonymous Q&A monitored for appropriate content
Newsletters—print and electronic
E-mails
School marquees
Parent/Teacher communiqués
Fundraising solicitations
Special Event mailings
Newspaper columns
Radio interviews
District cable channels
Senior citizen meal programs
Surveys
Partnership communiqués—PTA, business, foundations, clubs and organizations

Alumni newsletters
Targeted video presentations
Building tours—actual and virtual

Some districts are fortunate enough to employ an experienced communications coordinator or public relations director. These districts start The Great Conversation with a huge advantage. In-house PR professionals are already deeply involved in the outreach process, and they know the community. They are perfectly positioned to assume a central role in all phases of the formal track.[7] For those districts that lack a communications professional on their staff, I've found that the experts at the National School Public Relations Association (NSPRA) are willing and able to provide counsel and guidance on a wide range of communication issues. They can be a great source for ideas, materials, and technical support throughout all phases of the formal track.

Beyond the resources listed above, each district has additional, less obvious ways to spread the message. To identify these contextual channels, it is necessary to think broadly about all the ways the district "talks" with the public. For example, one feature of the environment that sends a powerful signal to the community is the appearance of the district's facilities. In their book, *Fixing Broken Windows*, James Wilson and George Kelling demonstrated that even small changes in the physical environment—for example, fixing windows and removing graffiti—resulted in significant, positive changes in public attitudes and behavior. It follows, therefore, that clean, dignified school buildings and surrounding grounds can encourage community confidence and support.

---

[7] In my experience, most PR professionals are excited by my recommendations and delighted by the prospect of a proactive, community-wide conversation. Most have been laboring for years to promote such a process, often in isolation. But please note: their presence on the staff should not be used as an excuse by senior management to dump the project on their desks and walk away. The formal track has been purposefully designed for a cross-section of district leaders to play an active role. One person in the communications office cannot and should not drive the process.

Samples of student work—strategically displayed throughout the community—also send positive messages to the public regarding curriculum, rigor, and achievement. It hardly matters whether the work is remarkable or routine. These public showings are intrinsically interesting and charming. Rotating exhibits can be placed in local businesses. Districts and local restaurants can partner to print placemats featuring student art, essays, homework, or, if we really want to start discussions, a typical history exam. Finding good material to display is never difficult. A cursory review of every teacher's student portfolios reveals a wealth of appropriate content. And like so many of the no-cost resources that are available within the district, student work exists in abundance. The more of it we place before the public—the more we show what students and teachers actually do—the more opportunities the public has to think favorably about their schools.

The most powerful weapon in our communications arsenal is also the most diabolical. I refer, of course, to the formal invitation bestowed upon an innocent member of the public to come in and shadow a teacher or an administrator for a day. Any civilian who manages to survive the experience automatically becomes an ally for life. This resource is available in every district, and I recommend its liberal use.

&CB

I offer these examples to prime the pump. The truth is that every school or district possesses a wealth of affordable communication tools, and new ones evolve all the time. People who are interested in participating in the formal track behind the scenes can contribute greatly by making sure that the power inherent in all these tools is harnessed, focused, and released into the community for maximum effect.

Once we have identified our potential resources, just one step remains in our preparation to take our message to the community. Using the information of our maps, we build a presentation schedule for Phase One.

Chapter 22

Creating a Comprehensive Schedule

Communication works for those who work at it.

John Powell

W e define the community's turf when we create our map. We both identify and conform to the community's convenience when we build our schedule.

Our goal here is simple: create a schedule that takes our teams to all the individuals and groups listed on our map when and where it's convenient for them to meet. The process is straightforward: call the designated contacts, explain The Great Conversation and its goals, and request an opportunity to make a presentation at their earliest convenience. With each call, we explain that this presentation is the first in an ongoing series focused on the topic of increasing student success and strengthening the community. This announcement places everyone on notice that something new has begun, and there is more to come.

It's important to keep in mind that every person in the community has a role to play in creating a culture of success, and anyone has the potential to become a "Hero of The Great Conversation" as the formal track unfolds. Having said this, it is smart—not to mention politically vigilant—to begin the scheduling process by contacting the community's most influential individuals and groups. In Phase One, the traditional power players and opinion leaders are best positioned to facilitate the rapid diffusion and acceptance of our message, so we call them first. After we have made these "priority" contacts, we proceed to schedule visits to all other groups.

Gaining access to the movers and shakers is usually easy; appointments can almost always be scheduled within the first weeks of the launch. Clubs and organizations that meet weekly are also easy to schedule. Program coordinators of these groups are usually desperate to find quality presentations, and they are quick to confirm a date. These folks are also delighted to learn that we intend to provide interesting, relevant content on an ongoing basis. Fortunately, many of the priority groups are in this category.

Groups that meet ten to twelve times per year offer a smaller window of opportunity. They have a tendency to book programs farther in advance, and it's likely that most will have time for no more than one presentation per year. The same holds true for those groups that have narrow agendas, such as book clubs, professional associations, or ethnic societies.

Please note that regardless of who we contact first, our presentations are always made on a "first available, first served" basis. This is key. Ideally, we would present our message to the power players first, but we never wait to speak to one individual or group because we have yet to speak to another whom we deem more important. The formal track is not a race, but, once we start, we want our message to a) quickly spread across the district's social networks, b) generate discussions throughout the community, and c) seep into the public's collective consciousness. We facilitate all three by speaking with everyone as soon as they are available to talk.

I acknowledge that scheduling according to the community's convenience makes it possible, indeed likely, that successive phases will overlap. We may, for example, be ready to launch Phase Two of our message before some groups have afforded us the op-

portunity to deliver Phase One. This is not a problem. Two phases can run simultaneously without confusion as long as we keep
track of our progress using our maps. It may seem unwieldy, but
the control we surrender by going to the community's turf at the
community's convenience is vastly outweighed by the control we
gain over the size of the turnout, the attention of the audience,
the tone of our presentations, and the content of our message. It's
an excellent bargain.

Chapter 23

A Second Front

*The void created by the failure to communicate is soon
filled with poison, drivel and misrepresentation.*

C. Northcote Parkinson

Every district, rich or poor, regardless of location, already has
the personnel, expertise, and resources it needs to map the
community, create a message, develop scripts, organize teams,
and build a schedule.

All that remains is to launch Phase One. And all we need to
launch is to have our teams show up for their first presentation,
share their message, and solicit a response. It is from the launch
of Phase One that we begin to dive deep into the community's
cultural matrix where nostesia and notions of "real school" are
found. This is when we begin to contrast perceptions with reality,
stimulate fresh insights, and foster an openness to change. With
that first presentation, we take a step toward the community, and
the people of the community take a step toward us. People begin
to comprehend that their interests are tied to the quality of their
schools. They start to see that their schools cannot meet the challenges they face alone. They begin to act as partners in the most
important enterprise of our time: moving our schools and our
students from where they are to where they need to be.

I am convinced that the formal track of The Great Conversation must play a central role in any effort to increase student success and every plan to prepare America's communities to prosper in the knowledge age. And I envision a day when everyone on staff and all their allies in the community eagerly volunteer to participate in this great endeavor. That day, however, is not now.

It is true that wherever I go there is a band of angels who embrace the call to be formally involved. They see the need, they understand the rewards, and they step right up to the line. To these people I say, "God bless you. Your students and the people of your community are in your debt. You will not have to wait to get to heaven to reap your rewards." But these intrepid warriors rarely represent more than a fraction of the staff. Everyone else falls into one of two groups.

Members of the first group have no interest in participating in any aspect of The Great Conversation. Some of them assert that it's "not in my contract." Others, including the T.T.S.P. crowd, make no pretense; they just walk away. I respect anyone's right to decline involvement in the formal track on any grounds, but I confess that these responses strike me as shortsighted and self-destructive. Anyone who invokes the limits of his or her job description fails to understand the growing threats to public education and, consequently, to his or her job security. Anyone who claims to have no professional or personal interest in the process fails to see how inaction puts those interests at risk. To these people, however, and to their senior administrators who may seek to impress their participation, I restate The Great Conversation's cardinal rule: it's voluntary. Everyone will always be welcome to join should they change their minds.

The second group to abstain from involvement is by far the largest—well over fifty percent of the staff. These folks get it: they accept the logic of The Great Conversation, and they understand the potential benefits. They have, however, no interest in being a part of the formal track. For some, it's the Biloski Syndrome on steroids: they are frazzled, overextended, and dancing as fast as they can. For others, it's partly a question of workload, but mostly a question of preference; they are not joiners. If they were to participate, it would have to be done in private, on their schedule, and on their terms.

To these people, I am pleased to report that there is a very effective way to contribute on *your turf*, at *your convenience*. You can operate within your personal social networks in the course of your normal routines. Participation adds next to nothing to your existing burden, and requires minimal change of lifestyle. By taking four simple steps, each person can accelerate the growth of understanding, trust, permission, and support. This second front of The Great Conversation was created to encourage universal participation. It's called the informal track.

Chapter 24

The Informal Track

*We must not, in trying to think about how we
can make a big difference, ignore the small daily
differences we can make which, over time, add up
to big differences that we often cannot foresee.*

Marian Wright Edelman

The informal track of The Great Conversation takes place privately within our individual social networks during the course of our daily routines. It adds nothing to the existing workload. The amount of time invested is entirely a matter of personal choice. The four action steps described below work so well because they are based on the power each individual has to influence his or her immediate environment. The steps are simple and practical. They add no pain. To the contrary: they produce joy.

The concept of the informal track was born in an Ohio school district. I was conducting a routine workshop designed to get people thinking about the Terrible Twenty Trends. I asked the group what had become my standard question: What's going on in American society to erode confidence in public education and drive the public away from public schools? As usual, a lively discussion ensued.

On this particular day, however, during a scheduled ten-minute break, I was chatting with a secretary who worked in the central office. Our conversation was playful. She was wearing a pin on her red sweater announcing her allegiance to "The" Ohio State University, and I, as a Penn State alum, was needling her about her football team's recent loss in Happy Valley, which I still have on my TiVo if anyone cares to see it. As the break ended, she said, "You know, not everything eroding public trust is going on out there in society. Some of it is going on right in here." Years before, I had learned to listen to school secretaries; they could be amazingly accurate in their assessment of their schools.

I thought about it for a minute, and then I did something as a presenter that is fraught with danger. I decided to go off script.

As soon as the group settled down, I posed a new question.

"Up to this point," I said, "you have identified some of the macroscopic social and economic trends causing the drift between the public and public schools. We have focused exclusively on external forces. Is it possible, however, that the people who work inside our schools are doing things to push the public away? Could it be that you are acting as your own worst enemies? Take fifteen minutes with the folks at your tables, then tell me what you've got."

The room exploded in discussion. I knew instantly I'd struck a nerve. The Buckeye gave me a wink from her chair.

The roar continued for fifteen minutes unabated. When I finally regained order and asked for their answers, nobody even bothered to raise a hand. They began shouting over one another. Everyone wanted to testify.

"We're defensive."

"We're arrogant."

"We fight about money in public."

"We blame everyone else for our problems."

"We don't listen very well."

"We give lip service to parental involvement."

"We don't care what the community thinks."

"We talk down to certain parents."

"We are vindictive."

"We resist change."

"We use too much jargon."

"We are too bureaucratic."

"We are not transparent."

"We wrap ourselves in tenure."

"We don't all live in the community."

"We all don't vote."

"We act like martyrs."

"We have a siege mentality."

"We think in term of us versus them."

"We wage turf battles in the media."

"We are isolated, inbred, and out of touch."

"We say we want partnerships, but we really only want money."

"We're in denial."

"We have weak relationships with our graduates."

"We think we can do it all by ourselves."

"We're reactive not proactive."

"We don't respond to the lies and half-truths."

"We distrust outsiders."

"We distrust each other."

"The professional staff talks down to the support staff."

"We enable bad parenting."

"We don't promote our success."

I have asked the question many times since, always to the same response. I call this the "Worst Enemies" list.

The value of the exercise was obvious right away. Besides the stimulating, perhaps cathartic effect that it had on the audience, the question "What are we are doing to make things worse?" shifted everyone's attention, including mine, to the role of the staff in shaping public opinion. Up to that point, my work had been focused on building an orchestrated, *collective* response to counter the external trends eroding public support, and the formal track had emerged from those efforts. But now it was clear that, in addition to the big cultural trends, there was something else to blame for declining support. The internal actions of a comparative few were pushing the public away. The secretary's remark, and the ruckus that followed, brought a new level of clarity. And as so often happens, as soon as I had the answer to one question, a new question arose: in addition to the formal track, what, if anything, can *individuals* do in their private lives to build the relationships we need?

Three weeks later, with this question still rolling around in my head, I sat in the audience at a business seminar at the Rosemont Theater in Chicago. It featured a program of prominent authors, scholars, and consultants representing various fields of business and marketing. None of these presenters had anything to do with public education or the school/community relationship. None of them knew me or my nascent ideas about the role of the individual in The Great Conversation. But as the house lights went down and I settled into my chair, it seemed that every presenter who took the stage was delivering a message written just for me.

John Naisbitt, the bestselling author of *Megatrends*, talked about the human craving for emotional authenticity in a frenetic, increasingly impersonal, techno-driven society. "Awash in high tech," he said, "we see a rising demand for high touch."

Dr. Lester Thurow, former dean at MIT, said that we were going to have to "change our culture" to retain our status as the world's preeminent power. "We have to talk to one another if we are going to change old attitudes. We must listen to one another in order to change the system." He was addressing the issue of global economic change, but everything he said could be easily applied to our schools.

Don Tapscott, a world-renowned authority on organizational transformation, discussed the need for "mass collaboration," a process in which individuals come together to share what they know and work together to improve a system.

Don Peppers, a marketing scholar, described his program for creating and maintaining profitable business relationships. He said, "You are going to have to engage your customers in a one-on-one *conversation* to build the relationships you need." I felt the hair on my arms stand up when he said it, because I swear he was staring right at me.

All things considered, it was quite a day.

Over the next few months, I repeated the "worst enemy" exercise in all my workshops, and the lists created were nearly identical. At the same time, I poured through marketing journals—an old habit from my ice cream years. Everywhere I looked I saw articles that spoke of the rising power of the individual to influence attitudes and behavior. The consensus was that this phenomenon was linked to media overload. Average Americans are exposed to over one million paid advertisements a year—everything from ads on matchbooks and billboards to the mega-ads of the Super Bowl. These commercials target our fantasies, our finances, and our bodies, and they are leaving no part untouched. This incessant selling merges with the 24/7 drone of "breaking news" and the blather of talking heads to create a cacophonous torrent of information, opinion, and hype. Marketing research indicates that we are responding by erecting mental filters to protect our brains from the clamor; we don't just doubt it all, we don't even hear it all. For years we've been turning inward, relying more on our own judgment, or looking to people we know and trust for guidance and advice.

In time, the feedback from my workshops fused with the cumulative data on word-of-mouth campaigns. Together, the two streams argued for something new: the creation of a second element that could run parallel to the collective activity of the formal track; a one-to-one approach that would tap the innate power each of us has to influence our family, friends, and neighbors; an informal track that anyone could easily join to help change the trends of time.

I was not sure exactly how to structure this second element, but I knew three things for sure about its ultimate design. First, it had to add nothing, or almost nothing, to the existing burden placed upon the people working in our schools. Second, it had to help secure the Prerequisites of Progress and neutralize the negative effects of the Terrible Twenty Trends. Third, it had to be personally satisfying—rewarding enough to encourage maximum participation by everyone on the staff. Creating an activity that would fulfill all three took some thinking, but I figured it out.

෨෬

The informal track of The Great Conversation has four steps. Like the formal track, all steps are doable and participation is voluntary. Unlike the formal track, the process takes place entirely on the individual's turf at the individual's convenience. Everyone can contribute, and I argue that everyone should. At the very least, everyone should take the first two steps. They are fulfilling, and easy.

Step One. Shift your attention to the positive.

Participation in the first step of the informal track requires us to do nothing. Well, almost nothing. We need to shift our attention from the negative to the positive.

This step is based on one of the few things that I have learned about the mystical workings of the universe: what we focus our attention on grows stronger in our life. If we constantly choose to focus on the negative things that occur in our classrooms, our schools, and our district, then we become more negative. Our psychology degrades. Optimism fades. Impatience and irritability grow. Our relationships suffer. We have less energy. Our health declines. By the end of the school year, we find ourselves questioning our purpose and doubting our value. Those who dwell on the negative are prime candidates for burnout.

Conversely, when we choose to put our attention on the hopeful, encouraging, positive developments that occur within our schools, we become more positive. Optimism grows. We feel energized. We feel better about ourselves as professionals and as human beings. Our relationships improve. We become more cheerful and productive, more awake, more actualized. Our health improves.

Making this subtle, internal shift—a small exercise in behavior modification—delivers all this and adds nothing to the existing workload.

I know the step is easy to trivialize in a society where immediate, concrete results are considered the true indicators of success. But, over time, the consequences of this step are real and quantifiable. If everyone on staff participates, the payoff is huge.

I would say that Ol' Bing was right when he sang, "You gotta accentuate the positive," but I've got a sinking feeling that many who read this will have no idea who Ol' Bing was.

Step Two. Stop bad-mouthing one another in public.

The second step of the informal track is not something we have to do, but something we have to stop doing. It is an act of omission. Teachers, paraprofessionals, support staff, administrators, and board members—*everyone*—must stop bad-mouthing one another and their schools in public. This is critical.

Bellyaching in public is not universal, but it is pervasive and highly destructive. It's the epitome of lose-lose behavior; it undermines the reputation of the speaker while simultaneously grinding down public opinion of local schools and public education as a whole. The teacher who stands in the grocery checkout line and criticizes her peers or the district spreads her negativity like a virus, and everyone within earshot is infected. She confirms their worst fears. She erodes their confidence in their schools. And although she does not intend it, she gives everyone who hears her negative rant permission to repeat it.

I'm not a bliss ninny. I know that many educators are shell-shocked and angry. They are appalled by their working conditions and bitter about the lack of respect they receive from students, parents, and the public. Millions resent being forced to raise America's kids, and they hate the hypercritical environment that surrounds them and the cynics who stoke the flames. They have reasons to complain. But venting in public is a nasty, destructive habit that hurts everyone and solves nothing. It must stop.

I'm not asking everyone to become saints or martyrs. There will be times when the fury and frustration become too much to bear. The pressure has to be released.

Fine. Go ahead. Gripe. But gripe to your spouse. That's why we have them.

Steps One and Two are potent, revolutionizing moves in and of themselves, and they add nothing to the existing burden. If everyone in the district did just these two things, the relationship between our schools and our communities would improve and everyone would benefit. But we can capitalize on our shift in attention, and exponentially increase our benefits, by taking the next step.

Step Three. Share something positive within your ego networks.

Everyone has an ego network. It's a personal social network comprised of family, friends, neighbors, and coworkers. Each of us sits in the center of our network as the "focal node," and we connect to the others in our networks through a web of "links" or "ties" in relationships ranging from close familial bonds to casual acquaintances. The size of our networks may vary, the connections we share may be weak or strong, but in every case our networks have real value. They provide social support, emotional and material aid, and companionship. In a world drowning in hype, we look to one another for honest information to discern the truth and make sense of the world. Networkees are predisposed to respect and trust one another.

This heightened level of mutual trust is a source of great power, and, from the perspective of the informal track, the most valuable feature of our networks. With just a little effort, we can harness this spirit of trust to expedite the movement of our message across our networks. And because each of our personal networks overlaps with hundreds of others, our individual efforts can accelerate the growth of understanding and trust throughout the entire community.

Even a casual reference to something positive—an allusion to some small breakthrough at school, the recounting of a hopeful moment with a student—added to our routine is enough to make an impression. The interpersonal dynamics are exactly the same as those set in motion by the bad-mouthing teacher in the checkout line, but the content of our remarks produces exactly the opposite effect: each positive impulse sets in motion a tiny wave of appreciation and goodwill. In isolation, these informal gestures may seem inconsequential, but as more and more of the people on staff share their positive experiences, thousands upon thousands of these coherent waves slide across hundreds of overlapping networks like ripples on a pond. As the waves interfere, they amplify. Soon, our positive comments and stories begin to permeate the public's awareness. The entire community is enlivened with good news about their schools, and everyone is energized in the process.

Step Three requires nothing more than sharing our personal stories, but we can do more. *If we are so inclined*, we can lace our informal discussions with references to the scripted message that is simultaneously being broadcast in the formal tract. There is no need to memorize the scripts or parrot the party line, but every teacher knows that repetition is fundamental to effective learning. With that in mind, we can accelerate the growth of understanding if we become familiar with the main points of the formal message and share them with our friends.

In the same vein, we should feel free to provide the people in our networks with examples of student work, including recent tests. (If a picture is worth a thousand words, an algebra exam is worth a million.) Assuming proper administrative approval, teachers might also consider exercising the "nuclear option," and ask friends and neighbors to become a teacher's aide for a day. It is true that this experience may forever scar the relationship, but nothing is more enlightening.

By choosing to take Step Three and share the message, each of us can leverage the power inherent in our networks. We can push back against the misinformation, disinformation, and outright lies that plague our schools. We can inoculate our friends against the viral negativity. On our turf, at our convenience, adding nothing to the existing workload, we can increase public support for our schools.

Step Four. Monitoring your progress.

Five minutes a week. That's all that is required to complete Step Four. In a quiet moment, perhaps in the relative calm of Sunday night before the race starts again, we need only ask ourselves, "How many times this week did I share something positive about my job, my class, or my school?" If you don't know the answer, guess. Precision is not required. Maybe the first time, the answer is six. Fine. Write it down or make a mental note, and pledge to do a little more in the coming week. Come next Sunday, ask the question again and record the answer with the intention to do better. That's all it takes to get a sense of where we have been with our message, and where we can go.

There is an "enhancement" to this step that, while not required, makes it easier to track our progress: we can create maps of our network. The process is similar to the mapping exercise performed in the formal track, but we map *our* turf instead of the community's. (There is a meticulous process called Social Network Analysis that yields elaborate webs of interlocking nodes and ties, but this isn't it.) Start by listing all the people with whom you interact in both your real and virtual worlds, then place each individual in one of three concentric circles. Close family and dear friends usually populate the center. Extended family and more casual friends, coworkers, and acquaintances occupy the second ring. Everyone else is in the third.

There is no need to labor over these lists. I have watched thousands of people in hundreds of workshops create their maps in less than thirty minutes, and just about everyone finds the experience to be rewarding, which is not a surprise. Few of us have taken the time to consider the breadth and depth of our social connections. The scope of our territory of influence can be an affirming revelation.

Once we have our network maps, using them is easy. In that moment of quiet reflection, we simply review our lists and place a check mark next to everyone with whom we shared some good news.

There are some people who take the monitoring step a bit further. They assign weights to each interaction based on the length and depth of the discussion. Of course, I'm pretty sure that the only people who go to this length were raised by mothers like mine. I doubt Mom was aware of B.F. Skinner and his experiments in operant conditioning, but she sure understood the power of extrinsic rewards. To this day I salivate when I see a star or a sticker made of shiny gold foil.

Monitoring with this level of precision is laudable, but not required. As stated above, taking five minutes to ask the basic question is sufficient. Our goals in Step Four are to gain a clearer picture of our progress and a new appreciation of the power each of us has to change our community. How aggressively we pursue these goals is a personal choice.

ℰℭ

The steps of the informal track outlined above are not exclusive. I'm sure many who read this will discover creative ways to improve the process. What's most important is that everyone finds a way to contribute. To do nothing while the Terrible Twenty Trends extinguish public trust is tragic. To go to school each day and grapple with the challenges heaped upon our schools and not push back even in some small way as Huns storm the gate is dangerous. It may reflect humility for educators to understate their victories, to keep to themselves the details of a week in which so much good was accomplished, but, in this environment, it is irrational.

Be advised that there may be those within our networks who resist our efforts. Certain family members will rush to argue. Some of our friends may spout maddening, mindless, mean-spirited rhetoric. That's okay. The informal track, like The Great Conversation as a whole, is not a test of wills. We're not trying to convince everyone that we are right and they are wrong. Our ultimate goal is to increase our community's support for student success. To that end, we are successful if all we do is take Step One and shift our attention from the negative to the positive. We are successful if all we do is stop bad-mouthing our coworkers, our students, and our schools in public. We are successful if we increase—even slightly—the amount of positive information flowing through our personal networks. We make a tremendous contribution to the welfare of our students and our community each time we stand up, tell our stories, and share some of what's right about our schools.

A final word about the informal track. I purposely developed the four steps to enliven, strengthen, and energize all who participate, and counter the forces that cause frustration, burnout, and despair. In that vein, I have a final word of advice for everyone who chooses to play a role. Relax.

Educators, especially teachers, have a tendency to try to do too much. Resist that inclination! If, at any point, taking any of the four steps becomes a strain, it's time to ease up. No one need struggle. It is true the stakes are high. We are trying to change America. To a considerable degree the future of public education depends on our success. It's a huge task, but no one should feel as though he or she must do it all. The people who work in America's public schools comprise one of the most powerful forces in the country, and in most places they are the largest employee group in the community. We will achieve our goals and everyone will benefit when we all comfortably do our part.

Chapter 25

The Return on Our Investment

*As soon as several of the inhabitants of the United
States have taken up an opinion or a feeling which they
wish to promote in the world, they look out for mutual
assistance; and as soon as they have found each other
out, they combine. From that moment they are no longer
isolated men, but a power seen from afar, whose actions
serve for an example, and whose language is listened to.*

Alexis de Tocqueville

I end Part IV the way I began. To get the schools we need, educators and their allies must initiate and maintain a positive
conversation with the communities they serve: a conversation that
runs on two tracks built to ensure maximum participation and
maximum progress.

I cannot lie. I wish I were proposing a more sophisticated
program to advance our goals. A proprietary package, perhaps,
containing slick videos, training manuals, and PowerPoint presentations; something I could sell to every school board in North
America for $20,000. Why? Because $20,000 x 15,000 districts
equals three hundred *million* dollars. Unfortunately, I'm not that
smart. After years of thinking and reading and working, I'm convinced the best approach is a low-tech, high-touch proposal that
costs nothing.

The fact that The Great Conversation requires little capital, however, does not mean that it offers paltry returns. The potential payoff is huge. Prerequisites of Progress, Plus!

The benefits begin to accrue as soon as Phase One is launched, starting with understanding. Each interaction raises the public's awareness of the challenges facing their schools. Adults who have long since left the classroom begin to grasp how much schools have changed. Community members begin to understand what it really means when they proclaim "teach all children to high levels," and they begin to get an idea of what it's going to take to accomplish this unprecedented goal.

With this knowledge comes the understanding that unfolding the full potential of every child is a shared responsibility. More and more people begin to see the big picture. Notions of private good and public good merge. An "I" mentality becomes a "we" mentality. Gradually, staff and community members develop a shared vision and a common language. Nostesia is reduced. Mental models are recast. It becomes abundantly clear to all that schools cannot do it alone. And, as has happened in American so many times before in times of crisis, people come together and create a new, more responsive community culture to tackle the task.

As community understanding grows, so do trust and respect. Each new point of positive contact helps educators and community members transcend stereotypes. People become more tolerant and empathetic. Relationships become more meaningful, less adversarial, and more productive. With each new presentation of student achievement, the public gains greater confidence in their schools. Teachers and administrators win greater trust in their ability to accomplish the goal. They also earn greater respect for who they are and what they do. Educators may not be able to take increased trust and respect to the bank (although maybe they can), but the intrinsic value of these benefits is priceless: they lubricate the wheels of progress; they foster cooperation and civility; and they increase professional (and personal) security in the face of uncertainty and change. Few educators I know would consider these benefits to be trivial.

Community permission to change flows naturally from increased understanding and trust. Interpreting just when permission is granted is more of an art than a science, but in time, The Great Conversation reveals a definite "sense of the community." Questions asked in the formal presentations display growing positivity and sophistication. Letters to the editor change in tone and content—the former becomes more rational, the latter more relevant. Opinion leaders who serve as bellwethers of public sentiment express a greater willingness to be engaged and supportive. All the ways that the community talks to itself and to its schools indicate that the overall tenor of the school/community relationship has improved. Bit by bit, change agents reach the point where they can assume with a reasonable level of certainty that their plans have been given a green light, or, at the very least, and not a red one. When that point is reached, when the requisite level of broad-based approval appears to be present, district leaders can press forward knowing they have enough political cover to survive the turmoil that always accompanies significant change. They and their allies on staff and in the community can safely advance toward the goal, confident that they have dramatically increased their chances of ultimate success.

The benefits of understanding, trust, and permission are rich and complete within themselves—a district would be glad to have any one in isolation. When present in combination, however, they generate the superbenefit of active community support. This support is expressed in two ways: direct and indirect.

Direct community support first appears in the form of increased public participation in school events, coupled with a greater flow of donated goods and services. Not long after the launch of Phase One, teachers and administrators discover they have access to a deeper pool of volunteers, mentors, and business partners. Increased opportunities for collaboration give everyone—staff, students, and community members—new ways to develop new skills and new interests. At the same time, district leaders who have struggled alone for years with helicopter parents, heavy-handed politicians, business bullies, and disgruntled community groups suddenly find themselves backed by a knowledgeable confederacy of allies: a rational group of citizens who possess the energy, resources, and political clout that all leaders need in good times and bad. Turnout climbs for school board elections, and the quality of candidates improves: they become more focused on the best interests of kids, as opposed to the best short-term deal for their neighbors. Over time, the enhanced quality of the board improves staff competence and morale. And finally, in those states where it applies, broad, sustained implementation of The Great Conversation drives up to record levels the number of "Yes" votes for bonds and levies. Community support can't get any more direct than that.

Indirect support flows to kids and schools in many streams, but they all originate from a single source: a pronounced rise in the community's store of social capital. Reciprocal feelings of goodwill and fellowship develop within The Great Conversation, and then spill into the wider community. In this atmosphere of heightened sociability, formerly disconnected individuals and groups begin to marshal their resources to remove the barriers that frustrate student success both in and out of school. Their combined efforts foster a rich, supportive, community-wide culture of achievement that envelops the community's youth.

A critical feature of this culture of achievement is the renewal of the home-school alliance. The support from home that teachers and administrators took for granted in the 1950s slowly begins to reemerge, and the benefits are keenly felt. Misbehavior in the classroom declines as parents, grandparents, aunts and uncles make it clear to their children that they support their teachers. Peer pressure is reduced, student indifference gives way to interest, even enthusiasm, as grown-ups take a more active role in promoting student progress. Children show up for school better prepared and with fewer problems as the "Holy Alliance" comes back into force.

So many prosocial benefits accrue when social networks are revitalized that an argument can be made that America's political leaders should do everything in their power to promote social capital stimulants like The Great Conversation in every state and community. The benefits generated are powerful predictors of student success—much more powerful than the imposition of standards, sanctions, national testing, or any other top-down regulatory approach, and they're free.

Beyond understanding, trust, permission, and support, the most significant benefit is a marked increase in approval of public schools. The Great Conversation delivers this extraordinary benefit by turning the common wisdom on its head.

It is widely reported that Americans are wavering in their support for public education because they are dissatisfied with student performance. If this is true, the prescribed antidote is obvious: improve student achievement and the public will re-embrace their schools and increase their support. The problem is that the common wisdom is wrong, and the proof is that the antidote does not work.

An honest analysis of disaggregated test results compiled over the last five decades shows a steady, albeit slow rise in student achievement in almost every ethnic, racial, and gender category. If the common wisdom were correct, then public satisfaction should have risen accordingly, but the opposite is true. And the reason is that the public is not moving away from their schools because they are dissatisfied, they are dissatisfied because they have moved away.

This conclusion seems wildly counterintuitive, but it's explained by David Mathews in his 1996 book, *Is There a Public For Public Schools?* Dr. Mathews, president and C.E.O. of the Kettering Foundation, traces the rise of dissatisfaction to the breakdown of the traditional school/community relationship. He concludes that the quality of the relationship that citizens have with their local schools directly affects their level of satisfaction with school performance. The stronger the relationship, the more satisfied they become. This is an incredibly important observation. It is completely consistent with my direct experience, and more importantly, it is supported by valid poll results.

Annual surveys by the Gallup Organization published in *Kappan* magazine reveal that the closer people are to their schools the more satisfied they become. For example, among all demographic groups, the one that gives its schools the highest approval rating is comprised of people who are very connected: parents with children in school. Within this group, however, there is a subgroup that's even more satisfied: parents with children in *elementary* school. Why? Because they are, by far, the most engaged. Conversely, the people who are least connected consistently give their schools the lowest marks. In other words, every step people take closer to their schools, the more they like what they see. The message is crystal clear: we have to get them closer. And that is exactly what The Great Conversation is designed to do. We bring members of the surrounding community closer to us by first taking a step toward them.

This does not mean that we should discontinue our efforts to increase student success. We must continue to do everything possible to improve student learning whether or not it improves public opinion. But by using both tracks of The Great Conversation to close the gap that has formed between our schools and our communities, we can enjoy the remarkable benefit of increased community satisfaction as we pursue the difficult goal.

ℴ∛

I am of the opinion that the benefits listed above are very much worth having. Schools will excel in districts where they are prevalent. Obstacles that retard student achievement will be removed. An environment that promotes innovation and progress will grow. Our friends, family, and neighbors will act as owners of their schools. Teachers and administrators will be accorded their proper status as the community's most important professionals. Children will become healthier, safer, and better educated. "Great Conversation Communities" will see their families, neighborhoods, and businesses thrive and prosper.

The Great Conversation can deliver all these results with minimal financial and human expense because de Tocqueville was right: when Americans combine in common purpose we are a power whose language is listened to. By adding this simple but essential ingredient, without breaking the budget, we can blunt the negative effects of the Terrible Twenty Trends, reinspire public confidence and trust, and enlist an army of allies ready to help us in our cause.

As with so many other life-altering endeavors, the most important thing we can do is take the first step. In this case, that means choosing to participate. We already have everything we need. We have a tremendous story to tell and an army of educated people to tell it. Each of us is already immersed in our own vibrant social networks that can act as conduits for our message. We are perfectly positioned to set the stage to unfold the full potential of every child. We can do this in every district. And we must do it now.

Chapter 26

A Most Hopeful Time

I believe that unarmed truth and unconditional
love will have the final word in reality.

Martin Luther King, Jr.

Everywhere I go I see educators working hard. This is one of two constants in my professional life these last twenty years. Millions of teachers, administrators, and the people who support them pour their hearts, minds, and bodies into the struggle each day.

I have watched thousands make the morning trek across the school parking lot. Their gait is confident and unassuming, a bit heavier perhaps in March than September. Teachers lug bulging satchels and ratty old canvas bags crammed with books, graded papers, and supplies, most of which they purchased at their own expense. They use these bags—freebees picked up at some conference—as counterweights as they yank open the heavy security doors and step across the threshold. They have entered the cloister. Most will have no contact with the outside world for the rest of the day. Once inside, they slide down familiar hallways and breathe in that singular smell: the pungent potpourri of chalk dust, floor polish, disinfectant, marker fumes, the lunch special, and the ever-present background tang emanating from the gym. It's the unmistakable smell of school. Eight out of ten Americans can identify that smell blindfolded.

After a few hasty greetings to coworkers, a mail stop, maybe an extra shot of caffeine, they enter their classrooms and stride to their desks. From this position they are, as Thoreau in the woods, monarchs of all they survey, except most have no control of the thermostat. In the stirring silence, they proceed with a few minutes of practiced preparation: a visual inspection of the room, an assignment written on the board, a quick inventory of available supplies.

It won't be long now. A dull roar is heard in the distance. Tramping feet grow louder in the hallway. They take a deep breath. Then comes the flood.

Fifty-three million school-aged children pour off the buses each day—eighty-eight percent of the nation's children age four to eighteen: the "raw material" of the educational process. It is the largest number of public school students in American history. All of them are bursting with potential. Many of them have physical, emotional, and cognitive problems that America's teachers and administrators have never seen before.

This teeming mass of diverse, distracted, demanding humanity requires constant attention from the opening bell, and most teachers spend their entire day on their feet literally immersed in the task. No time for phone calls. No time for collaboration. No time for reading or quiet reflection. From early morning to late afternoon, the vast majority of teachers run at full tilt with little time alone to take a breath. Of all the business leaders, media pundits, and politicians complaining about lazy teachers and their cushy jobs, not one has to carefully plan his entire day to make sure he has time to pee.

I don't know how they do it. I often wonder why they do it. Especially those who labor in dreadful conditions in schools whose existence in the richest country on Earth is a national disgrace.

I know that some are disheartened. I've spoken with teachers and administrators who are furious, shell-shocked, and holding on by their fingernails. I've met some who have gotten to the point where they don't like who they have become; they are tired and cynical, and I worry that, on some deep level, they have begun to believe the negative stereotypes that their critics perpetuate.

But the disillusioned are a minority. Most of the people who work in public schools get up day after day prepared and determined to make a difference. This remains true even though hundreds of thousands of America's educators have been labeled failures in the last eight years under No Child Left Behind. I would be completely demoralized if I was publicly chastised no matter how hard I worked. Yet, in a recent report by Public Agenda and Learning Point Associates, a significant majority of the teachers surveyed described themselves as happy and enthusiastic about the future. Eighty percent say they would choose the profession again if they were starting over, and most continue to hold fast to an abiding belief that all their students can learn to high levels when surrounded by proper support. In an enlightened society these heroic professionals would be compensated like rock stars and praised every day.

But they're not.

Instead of praise, America's educators find themselves ceaselessly criticized for their efforts. They are blamed for every dip in the economy, and yet never, ever praised during times of economic growth. They are blamed for low voter turnout, the general decline of civility, and rising crime rates—social maladies over which they have little or no control. Teachers, administrators, and board members are scorned as intransigent defenders of the status quo even though every program they implement and almost every procedure they follow has been developed, codified, and mandated by experts, politicians, and bureaucrats who rarely, if ever, step foot inside their schools.

This disdainful treatment is unjustified, shameful, and counterproductive. But the sad truth is that the criticism will continue, and the people who work in public schools will forever be identified as the problem until the underlying selecting premise of the education system is finally addressed.

Which brings me to the second constant in my journey: our schools need to change. We must replace the rigid, factory-like, time-based selecting system with a flexible, individualized, performance-based approach to learning if we are to produce the graduates we need. This was true when I arrived at the first Iowa Business and Education Roundtable meeting in 1988, and it is truer today.

For four decades, public schools have raised student achievement. Our teachers teach more children to higher levels in more subjects in more creative and dynamic ways than ever before. Only a handful of elite students in preceding generations knew as much as most kids know today. But, in spite of this remarkable success, every year the gap grows between what American students know and what they need to know to succeed as adults, and the reality is that American's educators cannot close this gap no matter how hard they work. They cannot develop high levels of functional literacy within every child, they cannot prepare all students for education beyond high school, they cannot deliver the results our nation needs. And it's not because they are lazy, stupid, arrogant, or unionized—their remarkable record of achievement in the face of unprecedented social change proves this.

No. America's teachers and administrators cannot meet society's expectations because these are outcomes that the selecting system was never designed to produce. The system we employ in almost every school—public and private—was not designed to create a nation of learners. It was designed to rake the genius from the rubbish. Its premise is based on false assumptions about the limits of learning and human intelligence. Its practices and procedures are deeply mired in concepts of an industrial society that no longer exists. It is neither efficient nor fair, and until we change the system, we guarantee that millions of young people will never enter the American mainstream, and every one of us will suffer as a result.

A detailed description of what must change, and what the new system, or, more likely, systems, should look like is the topic for another book, one not written by me. Many smart, dedicated professionals have worked on this complex issue throughout their entire careers. All I know for sure is that the schools we need must be built on the principle that the wealth of our nation is rooted in the brainpower, energy, and resourcefulness of our children—all of them. Schools of the knowledge age must be designed to enliven the total brain and develop the full creative intelligence of every child.

We can create these schools now. Everything we need has already been developed and tested in districts, schools, and classrooms across the country. The problem is not a lack of knowledge or proven programs. The problem is that the First Rule of School Restructuring applies: we cannot touch a school without touching the culture of the surrounding town. We cannot change the basic conditions in which teaching and learning occur without also changing America. Unfortunately, Americans have demonstrated, sometimes with a vengeance, that they will not permit a sweeping transformation of their schools—and their lives—just because their educators say they must. Before they will support the process, Americans must understand the issues, internalize the risks and rewards, and accept the need for change.

We must initiate and maintain The Great Conversation to secure the understanding, trust, permission, and support we need to achieve our goals. We must engage the people of our communities in a positive dialogue, on their turf, at their convenience, to mitigate the pernicious effects of the Terrible Twenty Trends. The Great Conversation—or something very much like it—must become a central feature of every district's efforts to increase student success, and now is an excellent time to start.

I know that it's not easy to see, but this is a blessed moment for America's public schools. For the first time in our history, two potent forces have converged—one moral, one practical—and their convergence presents us with an extraordinary opportunity.

The moral energy pours forth from a law of nature promulgated at the dawn of creation: each of us must do all we can do to help every child develop his or her full potential, starting with our own. If I had any doubt about the existence of this absolute directive, I was enlightened the night my son was born.

It had been a long day of labor. (I was exhausted!) The home birth we had meticulously planned with the midwife had been abandoned hours before when complications arose. At two-thirty in the morning, I was in an operating room watching as the C-section was performed. I stood transfixed. Awestruck. I don't remember breathing from the start of initial incision to the moment the doctor put down his tools, leaned forward, and reached his hand into the gap. With a deft pull, he lifted something out.

It was a boy, and he was perfect. Not all squished and smashed by contractions in the birth canal. Not covered with mucus and meconium. Perfect. A perfectly shaped head. A beautiful color. Dark, wispy curls. Perfectly silent and beautiful, with two blazing eyes looking right into mine.

And in that moment, I heard a message. No one will ever talk me out of this. I heard a message, and the message was from God, or someone very close. It was not verbal. It was visceral. It shot through every fiber of my being, and it was crystal clear.

"Here is your child. He's a gift. Your job now is to do all you can do to help him realize his full potential."

It was not a suggestion. It was a command, and whether heard or felt or somehow missed, this universal command is issued each time a child comes into the world.

I believe strongly that the parents of each child bear the primary responsibility for fulfilling this moral imperative. But I also believe that this obligation has a bright penumbra that extends to all of us. We are each called upon to help remove the impediments to achievement for every child regardless of race, gender, or ethnic background, and we know it. The impulse to help is encoded in our DNA; some biologists maintain that it is the essence of human nature. This deep drive spurs total strangers to come to a child's aid in times of crisis. It's especially lively in the hearts of teachers. It spurred Miss Skelton to reach out and give a lost young redhead a great education—an act my father would never forget; a gift that changed the fortunes of his family for generations.

To raise up each child, to refuse to allow his or her achievement to be limited by factors that are remediable, this has always been the moral course. But we've never done it. Not for every child.

Why?

Because it was never practical. And while it is true that Americans are a decent and moral people, we tend to be a bit more practical than moral, especially when we can invent a plausible or moderately implausible justification for our actions. In this case, it was easy. For the truth is that we didn't need them all. For over two hundred years, to succeed as a people we needed to teach only a small fraction of America's children to high levels, and so that's what we did. And we invented convenient rationales of fairness and ideologies of bell curves to take us off the hook.

And we could and would continue with this ruse today were it not for the demise of the industrial age. We now *need* to unfold the full potential every child, and except in the most cosmic sense, morality has nothing to do with it. Human capital has become that key factor in the competitive formula around which all other factors revolve. Our prosperity, our security, and our social tranquility now depend, as never before, upon our ability to help all children discern and develop their innate resources—to do everything that we can to help all children acquire the knowledge and skills they need to thrive in the global society.

The words of Jefferson's original mandate still apply: we must educate each child *"well enough"* to be able to transact his business and participate in the civic life of his community. Centuries later, the basic charge remains the same, but the expanded meaning of those two little words has changed everything. Everyone must now be raised up to be a learner. The thrust of history has merged the moral imperative with our practical need, and this alignment is producing a mighty stream of energy that we can harness to create the schools we need.

This is a moment set apart. We must grab hold of it and lay our case before the public. We must help the people of our communities understand that their schools must change. We must help them see that everyone will directly benefit from these changes, whether or not they have children in school. Our formal presentations must show that it's in the community's interest to remove all the obstacles to student achievement; that everyone, privileged or poor, young or old, will benefit by working to ensure that no child is denied the physical, social, psychological, or emotional support he or she needs to progress. Our informal discussions must help the members of our social networks see that their schools cannot do it alone: they cannot prepare all students in mind, body, and spirit well enough to thrive in the knowledge society without everyone's support.

And in both tracks of The Great Conversation, we must take every opportunity to tell public education's remarkable story of success. We must make it clear that we have the most open, responsive, and effective public schools in the world. We must show the public that their schools are centers of exploration, innovation, opportunity, and achievement. In every interaction, we must remind the people that public schools were created to make our democracy a reality. For centuries they have been indispensable in the creation of the most free, creative, and powerful country on the planet, and they remain the principal mechanism through which this nation makes good on its fundamental promise of liberty, justice, and opportunity for all. This is the truth. It is the quintessential American message, and Americans want to hear it.

ℰℭ

I entered the public education arena as a critic with grand convictions and blistering rhetoric. Twenty years later, my trip through the land of blueberries, bell curves, and Betty Jo has left me covered with battle scars, but excited about the future and convinced that the best is yet to come. I am aware of the threats. I have seen firsthand the many ways that public education is under attack. I know that America's educators are working in uncharted territory facing ever-increasing expectations with insufficient resources. But I also know that America has never needed a highly educated citizenry more. Every path to individual, community, and national success runs through those wide-open classroom doors. Schools cannot do it alone. But conditions are finally right for all Americans to do their part. To join together in common purpose and help their educators create the schools we need, and, simultaneously, build the communities of our most noble dreams. Public education *is* a miracle, and this is its most hopeful time.

Acknowledgements

My first thought was, "I'll just write an expanded version of my keynote address." I wrote the first three pages in twenty minutes. The words flowed easily across the screen. At the end of an hour, I was convinced I would complete the book in twelve months— eighteen max.

Seven years later, I delivered the finished file to the editor. In the interim, I have written and rewritten those first words many times. Beginning with an outline would have been a good idea.

I was sustained throughout the process by the interest and enthusiasm of many friends and colleagues. In a very real sense, every school district, professional association, community college, education foundation, educational service center, and chamber of commerce that invited me to speak became part of a feedback loop that both informed and encouraged my work. Every teacher, administrator, and board member who approached me at the end of a talk to ask, "Have you written a book?" raised the internal pressure, without which I might never have reached the end. I am in their debt.

Among these individuals and groups there are some who deserve my special thanks. In my professional life, those who were especially supportive among school boards include the leaders of the Kentucky, Michigan, Utah, Washington, and West Virginia School Board Associations. Among administrators were the executive directors and staffs of the Arkansas, Arizona, Colorado, Maine, Oregon, and Texas associations of school administrators, especially the Texas Association of Secondary School Principals. I am indebted to many of the state teachers' organizations, but particularly the people at Education Minnesota, and the education associations of Washington and Pennsylvania. At the national level, I have enjoyed the continued support of the National School Boards Association, including Anne Bryant and her staff; the leaders of the American Association of School Administrators, especially Bruce Hunter; the people at the National Association of Secondary School Principals, especially Dr. Tirozzi; the staff at the National Association of Elementary School Principals; and leaders, past and present, of the National Education Association. The senior staff at the National School Public Relations Association, especially Rich Bagin, provided me with information, confidence, and encouragement.

I owe a great deal to the capable staffs and dedicated volunteers at the National PTA and the North Central Educational Research Laboratory. Much of what I learned of the history of education and the power of individuals to effect change I discovered during my time as a board member of these groups.

By virtue of our extended interactions, some of my professional relationships evolved into friendships. First and foremost, I must acknowledge the Iowans, starting with William Lepley, Iowa's former Director of Public Instruction. From the moment he asked me to serve on the Iowa Business and Education Roundtable, Bill helped me become a more thoughtful and effective advocate for the creation of world-class public schools. He, his deputy Ted Stillwell, and the staff at the Department in Des Moines completely changed my life for the better. Across town, all of the people at the Iowa State Education Association, especially Fred Comer, Angie King, and Gerald Ott, treated me with great patience, and there were times in the early years when that must have been an effort. The same can be said for Gaylord Tryon and the leaders at the School Administrators of Iowa. Ron Fielder, CEO of the Grant Wood Area Education Agency, was a friend and adviser from the beginning.

Acknowledgements

Beyond Iowa, I am grateful for the relationships I established with the staff, board, and community members of Mesa District 51 in Grand Junction CO. And I will forever be in debt to two people in southwest Wisconsin, Greg Quam at Platteville High School and Darla Burton at CESA #3 in Fennimore. Their continued interest in this book over the last nineteen months acted as a light at the end of the tunnel during dark moments of doubt.

Not surprisingly, it is the people in my personal life who provided the most immediate and uninterrupted support, and it is to them I owe the most. Were it not for Josh Roberts, this book might not exist. It was he who convinced me that I had something to say. My dearest friend Laurie Sluser was, as always, a wellspring of positive energy and practical insight; his contributions to everything from the content of the text to the design of the cover made the finished product better throughout. My next-door neighbor Steve Terry provided the invaluable service of keeping me from being stuck inside my head. His running commentary on human genetics, Jungian archetypes, and the planting of trees was a constant, and necessary, source of stimulation. My friends Frank Wintroub and Todd Burkhardt gently, but repeatedly, reminded me that I had to set a deadline or else the book would never get done. I managed to ignore them for months on end, but I have no doubt that they facilitated the process. My friend Dean Draznin took every opportunity to tell me that I was writing a great book, and that it would sell—a lot. I was too anxious to take his predictions seriously, but I never got tired of hearing them.

And then there is my wife, Jeanne, who has been improving my work since we were twenty years old. She spent the last two years living with a madman who was constantly consumed with whatever passage he was writing, and talking about each one over and over again. This says nothing of her having to abide my moods as they soared, sometimes hourly, between exuberance and despair. She never complained. Her enthusiasm for the project never wavered. Her confidence in my abilities was always on display. If that were not enough, she brought a deep, intuitive understanding of the issues presented in these pages, and an uncanny ability to point me in the right direction when I had lost my way. This book would not be nearly as coherent, and my life would be poorer in every way, without her intimate and committed involvement.

Selected Bibliography

Adler, Mortimer J. "The Crisis in Contemporary Education." *The Social Frontier,* February 1939, 140–145.

Baker, Keith. "Are International Tests Worth Anything?" *Phi Delta Kappan,* 89 (2), October 2007, 101–104.

Bell, J. Carleton. "The Historic Sense." *Journal of Educational Psychology,* May 8, 1917, 317–18.

Berliner, David C., and Bruce J. Biddle. *The Manufactured Crisis: Myths, Fraud, and the Attack on America's Public Schools.* Reading, Mass.: Addison-Wesley, 1995.

Berliner, David C. "Our Impoverished View of Educational Reform." *Teachers College Record,* August 2, 2005.

Berryman, Sue E., and Thomas R. Bailey. *The Double Helix of Education and the Economy.* New York: Institute on Education and the Economy, Teachers College, Columbia University, 1992.

Boyer, Ernest L. *The Basic School: A Community for Learning.* Princeton, N.J.: Carnegie Foundation for the Advancement of Teaching, 1995.

Bracey, Gerald W. *Setting the Record Straight: Responses to Misconceptions about Public Education in the United States.* Alexandria, Va.: Association for Supervision and Curriculum Development, 1997.

—. "April foolishness: The 20th anniversary of A Nation at Risk." *Phi Delta Kappan, (84)* April 8, 2003, 616–621.

Brady, Marion. "The Education Reform Train Is Off the Track." *Washington Post,* December 23, 2009.

—. "Bucking Conventional Wisdom." *The School Administrator,* September 2006.

Callahan, Raymond E. *Education and the Cult of Efficiency,* Chicago: University of Chicago Press, 1962.

Chubb, J. and Terry Moe. *Politics, Markets, and America's Schools.* Washington, D.C.: Brookings Institution, 1990.

Comer, James P. *Waiting for a Miracle: Why Schools Can't Solve Our Problems—and How We Can.* New York: Penguin, 1997.

—. "An Open Letter to the Next President." *Education Week.* Vol. 27 (19), January 16, 2008.

Connors, Robert J. and Andrea A. Lunsford. "Frequency of Formal Errors in Current College Writing, or Ma and Pa Kettle Do Research." *College Composition and Communication*, Vol. 39, (4), December 1988, 395–409.

Cremin, L. *The Transformation of the School: Progressivism in American Education, 1876-1957.* New York: Knopf, 1961.

—. *American Education: The Metropolitan Experience, 1876-1980.* New York: Harper & Row, 1988.

Darling-Hammond, Linda. *The Right to Learn: A Blueprint for Creating Schools That Work.* San Francisco: Jossey-Bass, 2001.

Deal, Terrence E. and Kent Peterson. *Shaping School Culture: The Heart of Leadership.* San Francisco: Jossey-Bass, 1999.

Doidge, Norman. *The Brain That Changes Itself.* New York: Penguin, 2007.

Druker, Peter. *Post-Capitalist Society.* New York: Harper-Collins, 1993.

Elicker, Paul. "Let's Speak the Truth About Our Schools." *National Association of Secondary School Principals Bulletin*, Vol. 42, 1968, 1–10.

Finn, Chester E. *Troublemaker: A Personal History of School Reform Since Sputnik.* Princeton: Princeton University Press, 2008.

Florida, Richard. *The Rise of the Creative Class.* New York: Basic Books, 2002.

Fullan, Michael. *Leading in a Culture of Change.* San Francisco: Jossey Bass, 2003.

—. "School Leadership's Unfinished Agenda." *Education Week*, Vol. 27 (32), April 9, 2008.

Galbraith, John Kenneth. *The Good Society.* Boston: Houghton Mifflin, 1996.

Gardner, Howard. *Frames of Mind: The Theory of Multiple Intelligences.* New York: Basic Books Inc., 1983.

—. *The Disciplined Mind: What All Students Should Understand.* New York: Simon and Schuster, 1999.

Gatto, John Taylor. *Dumbing Us Down: The Hidden Curriculum of Compulsory Schooling.* Philadelphia: New Society Publishers, 1992.

Gerstner, Louis V. "Our Schools Are Broken," *New York Times.* May 27, 1994. A-27.

Gladwell, Malcolm. *The Tipping Point.* New York: Little Brown, 2000.

Greer, Colin. *The Great American School Legend: A Revisionist Interpretation of American Education.* New York: Basic Books, 1972.

Hanifan, Lyda. "The Rural School Community Center," *Annals of the American Academy of Political and Social Science* 67, 1916, 130–138.

Hatch, Thomas. *Managing to change: How schools make improvements in turbulent times.* New York: Teachers College Press, 2009.

Hirsch, E.D. *Cultural Literacy: What Every American Needs to Know.* Garden City, NY: Vintage, 1988.

—. *The Schools We Need: And Why We Don't Have Them.* Garden City NY: Anchor, 1999.

Hodgkinson, H. "Why have Americans never admired their own schools?" *The School Administrator.* Vol. 53, 1996.

Howard, Phillip K. *The Death of Common Sense: How Law is Suffocating America.* New York: Random House, 1994.

Johnson, J. and J. Immerwahr. *First Things First: What Americans Expect from Public Schools.* New York: Public Agenda Foundation, 1994.

Kohn, Alfie. *The Case Against Standardized Testing: Raising the Scores, Ruining the Schools.* Portsmouth, N.H.: Heinemann, 2000.

Kozol, J. *Savage Inequalities: Children in America's Schools.* New York: Crown, 1993.

Lakoff, George. *Don't Think of an Elephant: Know Your Values and Frame the Debate.* White River Junction: Vermont, 2004.

Latane, Bibb and John M. Darley. *The Unresponsive Bystander: Why Doesn't He Help?* Englewood Cliffs, N.J.: Prentice-Hall, 1970.

Levin, H., C. Belfield, P. Muennig, and C. Rouse. *The Costs and Benefits of an Excellent Education for All of America's Children.* New York: Teachers College, Columbia University, 2006.

Levin, Ben. "The Failure of Failure." *Phi Delta Kappan,* November 1, 2007.

Levine, Arthur E. "Waiting for the Transformation." *Education Week.* Vol. 28 (22), February 25, 2009.

Martin, Michael T. "A Strange Ignorance: The Role of Lead Poisoning in Failing Schools." Retrieved from http://www.azsba.org.

Marzano, Robert J. and John Kendall. *Essential Knowledge: The Debate Over What American Students Should Know.* Aurora, CO: McREL, 1999.

Mathews, David. *Is There A Public For Public Schools?* Dayton, OH: Kettering Foundation, 1996

—. *Reclaiming Public Education by Reclaiming Our Democracy.* Dayton, OH: Kettering Foundation, 2006.

Mathews, Jay. *Class Struggle: What's Wrong (and Right) with America's Best Public High Schools.* New York: Three Rivers Press, 1999.

Meehan, Mary, Larry Samuel, and Vickie Abrahamson. *The Future Ain't What It Used To Be.* New York: Riverhead Books, 1998.

Meier, Deborah. "Educating for What? The Struggle for Democracy in Education." *Power Play*, 1(1), 2009, 20–28.

Meier, Deborah and Diane Ravitch. "Bridging Differences." *Education Week*. Vol. 25 (38), May 24, 2006.

Mishel, Lawrence, Jared Bernstein, and Heidi Shierholz. *The State of Working America 2008/2009*. Economic Policy Institute, 2008.

Mishel, Lawrence. "The Exaggerated Dropout Crisis." *Education Week*. Vol. 25, Issue 26, March 8, 2006: 40.

Moore, Stephen and Julian L. Simon, *It's Getting Better All the Time: Greatest Trends of the Last 100 Years*. Washington, D.C.: Cato Institute, 2000.

Nichols, S. and T. Good. "Why today's young people are viewed so negatively (And why they shouldn't be)." *Education Week*. Vol. *23*(31), April 14, 2004.

Ohanian, Susan. *One Size Fits Few: The Folly of Educational Standards*. Portsmouth, NH: Heinemann, 1999.

Padover, Saul K. *Jefferson: A Great American's Life and Ideas*. New York: Harcourt, Brace & World, 1952.

Perelman, Lewis J. *School's Out: Hyperlearning, the New Technology, and the End of Education*. New York: Morrow, 1992.

Poterba, James M. "Demographic Structure and the Political Economy of Public Education." *National Bureau of Economic Research Working Paper Series, Paper No. 5677*, (July 1996).

Putnam, Robert D. *Bowling Alone: The Collapse and Revival of American Community*. New York: Simon & Schuster, 2000.

Ravitch, Diane. *Left Back: A Century of Battles over School Reform*. New York: Simon & Schuster, 2001.

—. "Why I Changed My Mind About School Reform" *Wall Street Journal*, March 9, 2010.

Ries, Al and Jack Trout. *Bottom-Up Marketing*. New York: McGraw-Hill, 1989.

Rifkin, Jeremy. *The End of Work: The Decline of the Global Labor Force and the Dawn of the Post-Market Era*. New York: Putnam, 1995.

Riley, Richard. The state of education address. Washington, D.C. 1996.

Rotberg, Iris C. "Quick Fixes, Test Scores, and the Global Economy." *Education Week*. Vol. 27. (41) June 11, 2008.

Rothstein, Richard. *The Way We Were? The Myths and Realities of America's Student Achievement*. New York: Century Foundation Press, 1998.

Schlechty, Phillip C. *Schools for the 21ˢᵗ Century: Leadership Imperatives for Educational Reform*. San Francisco: Jossey-Bass, 1990.

—. *Leading for Learning: How to Transform Schools into Learning Orga-*

nizations. San Francisco: Jossey-Bass, 2009.

Seeley, David. "A Report's Forgotten Message: Mobilize." *Education Week*. Vol. 28 (22), February 25, 2009.

Senge, Peter. *The Fifth Discipline: The Art & Practice of the Learning Organization*. New York: Doubleday, 1990.

Sizer, Theodore R. *Horace's School: Redesigning the American High School*. Boston: Houghton Mifflin, 1992.

Smith, Daniel A. *Howard Jarvis' Legacy? Assessing Anti-Tax Initiatives in the American States*. Abstract. Department of Political Science, University of Denver, 2002.

Thurow, Lester C. *Building Wealth: New Rules for Individuals, Companies, and Nations in a Knowledge-Based Economy*. New York: Harper Business, 1999.

—. *Fortune Favors the Bold: What We Must Do to Build New and Lasting Global Prosperity*. New York: Harper Collins, 2003.

Tienken, C. "The study of test scores and economic competitiveness." *International Journal of Education Policy and Leadership*, Vols. 3 & 4, April 25, 2008.

Tyack, D. *The One Best System*. Cambridge, MA: Harvard University Press. 1974.

Walker, Samuel. *The Rights Revolution: Rights and Community in Modern America*. Oxford University Press US, 1998.

Wat, Albert. "Dollars and Sense: A Review of Economic Analyses of Pre-K." *Pre-K Now Research Series*, May 2007.

Whittle, C. "Lessons learned: the Edison project founder's musings on American schooling." *The School Administrator*. 54, 1997.

A Matter of Time: Risk and Opportunity in the Nonschool Hours. Report of the task force on youth development and community programs. Carnegie Corporation of New York, 1992.

"College Bound Seniors." Total Group Profile Report. The College Board. 2007.

Essential Components of a Successful Education System. National Business Roundtable, 2000.

"Ignorance of U.S. History Shown by College Freshmen." *New York Times*. April 4, 1943.

The Writings of Thomas Jefferson. Memorial Edition. 20 Vols. Edited by Andrew Lipscomb and Albert Bergh. Washington, D.C.: Thomas Jefferson Memorial Association 1903.

What Matters Most: Teaching for America's Future. Report of the National Commission on Teaching & America's Future. New York. 1996.

"Public schools: Do they outperform private ones?" *Christian Science Monitor,* May 10, 2005.

"Times Test Shows Knowledge of American History Limited." *New York Times.* May 2, 1976.

"We Are Less Educated than 50 Years Ago." *U.S. News & World Report,* 30 November 1956, 68–82.

"What Went Wrong with U.S. Schools." *U.S. News & World Report,* 24 January 1958, 68–77.

United States Government Publications

"120 years of American Education: A Statistical Portrait." National Center for Education Statistics. Washington, D.C.: U.S. Department of Education, 1993.

Cahalan, M.W., S. J. Ingels, L. J. Burns, M. Planty, and B. Daniel. "United States High School Sophomores: A Twenty-Two Year Comparison, 1980-2002." National Center for Education Statistics, Washington, D.C.: U.S. Department of Education, 2004.

"Condition of Education Report 2004." National Center for Education Statistics. Washington, D.C.: U.S. Department of Education, 2005.

"Condition of Education Report 2007." National Center for Education Statistics,Washington, D.C:. U.S. Department of Education, 2008.

"Digest of Education Statistics 2005." National Center for Education Statistics, Washington, D.C.: U.S. Department of Education, 2006.

"Drop Out Rates in the United States 2005: National Completion Rates." National Center for Educational Statistics. Washington, D.C., 2007.

"Drop Out Rates in the United States 2005. National Completion Rates." National Center for Educational Statistics. Washington, D.C.: U.S. Department of Education, 2007.

Kirsch, Irwin S., Ann Jungeblut, Lynn Jenkins, and Andrew Kolstad. "Adult Literacy in America: A First Look at the Results of the National Adult Literacy Survey." National Center for Education Statistics, Washington, D.C., September 1993.

"Percentage of the Population 3 Years Old and Over Enrolled in School, by Age, Sex, Race, and Hispanic Origin: October 1947 to 2005." U.S. Department of Commerce, Bureau of the Census, Current Population Survey, Table A-2. 2007.

"Percentage of High School Graduates Completing a Core Academic

Curriculum." *Digest of Education Statistics 2005,* Tables 135, 141. National Center for Educational Statistics. Washington, D.C.: 2006.

"Prekindergarten in U.S. Public Schools: 2000-2001." National Center for Education Statistics. Washington, D.C.: U.S. Department of Education, 2003.

Prisoners of Time. Report of the National Education Commission on Time and Learning, U.S. Government Printing Office, 1994.

"Report of the Committee of Ten on Secondary School Studies: Appointed at the meeting of the National Educational Association July 9, 1892, with the reports of the conferences arranged by this committee and held December 28-30, 1892." Washington, Government Printing Office. 1893.

"Schools and Staffing Survey 1999-2000." National Center for Education Statistics. Washington, D.C.: U.S. Department of Education, 2002.

"U.S. Census Bureau Household and Family Characteristics, Detailed Tables for Current Population Report p 20-515, Tables 16, 17 and 18, "Households, by Type, Age of Member, Age, Sex, Race, and Hispanic Origin of Householder." Current Population Survey Report, March 1998.

"United States High School Sophomores: A Twenty-Two Year Comparison, 1980-2002." National Center for Educational Statistics. Washington, D.C.: September 2006.

What Matters Most: Teaching for America's Future. National Commission on Teaching and America's Future, September 1996.